DUPED!
Deception in Graceland

SARA LANG

DUPED! Deception in Graceland

Copyright © 2012 by Sara Lang

Walnut Fork Press

P.O. Box 7201, St. Petersburg, Florida 33734

All rights reserved. This book or any portion thereof may not be reproduced or used in any manner whatsoever without the express written permission of the publisher. Excerpts and quotes may be used without permission as the US Fair Use Act allows.

Printed in the United States of America

Cover Design: Wheres?Amanda

First Printing, 2012

Library of Congress Control Number: 2012931759

ISBN-13: 978-0-615-59578-8

Additional copies may be purchased through amazon.com and other retailers

Scripture taken from The New King James Version. Copyright © 1982 by Thomas Nelson, Inc. Used by permission. All rights reserved.

All web addresses are current with the publication date of this book. They, of course, are subject to change without notice.

With love and gratitude for my Lord

And the faithful family

He has given me

PREFACE

Duped! Misled by an insidious deception in the faith by which I've walked since the age of seven? Now retired, I reflect on the inner expectation I've always had that I would live to experience these "last days," being aware of Jesus' forewarning in the Gospel According to Matthew.

> For then there will be great tribulation, such as has not been since the beginning of the world until this time, no, nor ever shall be. And unless those days were shortened, no flesh would be saved; but for the elect's sake those days will be shortened. Then if anyone says to you, "Look, here is the Christ!" or "There!" Do not believe it. For false christs and false prophets will arise and show great signs and wonders, so as to deceive, if possible, even the elect. See, I have told you beforehand" (Matthew 24:21-25).

Being aware, then, of Jesus' urgent admonition for His followers to be vigilant, how could it be that an active and believing Christian of fifty-nine years would be one of the "deceived?" The loving words of Jesus, "See, I have told you beforehand," gave the comfort of His protection for His own.

My trek in the quest to discover what was going on began with research on the rapidly developing interfaith movement. This led to "emerging church" books and websites. As I further delved into the phenomenon of the emerging church, I realized that my husband and I were in one! There were things with which we did not fully agree or understand, but we trusted so much in the pastor, that we let these things slide in our minds. Upon continued research, the basic reasons for areas of concern were found. The answers were embedded in the books written by emergent church leaders. After reading many books, and researching various websites, the conclusion was drawn that we should share what we've learned.

In pursuit of the foundational beliefs which came to fruition in the emerging church, it was an astounding discovery that the roots of all that concerned us were to be found in New Age / New Spirituality doctrine. It was apparent that the New Age we had heard about in the 70's and 80's had reappeared and been repackaged for Christian consumption! Several of the chapters in *Duped* will include information entitled, "Sleight of Hand" vocabulary. There you will view common words and phrases found not only in the Holy Bible, but also slyly tucked in New Age terminology and belief.

The information in this book is vital to people of all ages, especially those who desire to see the concepts of the Bible compared to present postmodern thinking. "Chapter Questions For Reflection," in Appendix A, will stimulate further discussion and study. I'm sharing this project in "blog format," in order to highlight questions and research in an "easy read." I am hoping that readers will put themselves into the blog conversations, creating a starting point for further individual research and discussion.

- Sara Lang

INTRODUCTION

Have you ever heard someone say, "I like Jesus ... I just don't like "the church?" Maybe that was even your own inner voice you heard talking! This restless attitude coupled with the pluralistic culture, by which we're quickly being tinted, could just land us in an emerging church. What is the postmodern, emerging church, sometimes referred to as the emergent church? I will use the terms interchangeably since the bedrock of all three is indicative of the same principles.

Generally, an emerging church is a veiled, illusive "conversation" among people in this postmodern age. It is a response to the quest for "spirituality," attempting to address, or perhaps disregard, the question of theology in our culture of relativity. It follows that each community (formerly called church) is in a constant flux as to how it sees theology, accuracy of scripture, exclusiveness of Jesus Christ as the only Savior, and the atonement issue. Therefore, it is purposely impossible to "nail down" an answer to, "What is the emergent church?" Generally, the postmodern church is not strong on "getting saved," "defining sin," "choosing heaven or hell as an informed response each of us will make," or "accepting the Bible alone as the inerrant all-powerful Word of God." "Experience designers" (formerly called pastors) lead in uniquely variant paths designed to meet the specific needs of the sub-cultures they serve. The name of the game: Become one with the culture around you, then evolve through an ever-changing theology in order to meet the vision and desires of that culture.

Beginning in the 1990's, "rapid change" became the buzz word for all infrastructural systems, including education, government, politics, economics, health care, and yes, even the church. Those in positions of authority in these realms were and are known as "change agents." As demonstrated by the paragraph above, we are to meet the "new" ideas with "new" methods and "new" frameworks for theology. Just as in education, "experience trumps knowledge" in our postmodern era.

God's Word of "salvation by grace in faith alone" will take a back seat to systems of works and rituals delivered to us by ancient mystical practices.

Coming alongside these changes is an interfaith push toward unity with other world religions. The Overton Window is sliding uncharacteristically fast as many systems are scurrying to take their places in our globally united world. Those who oppose this global pressure will be viewed as resisters to a "one-world spirituality and global peace" (Oakland 13). Roger Oakland, in *Faith Undone*, explains, "A common technique to changing society (or the church) is to repeat an assertion over and over as fact; once people have heard a statement enough times, they come to believe it is true" (Ibid.). This is a good time to interject the apostle Paul's warning to the church at Thessalonica: "Prove all things; hold fast to that which is good" (1 Thessalonians 5:21).

The Emerging Church, written by Dan Kimball, presents comments on the present global world with so many different religions: "In a post-Christian world, pluralism is the norm. Buddhism, Wicca, Christianity, Islam, Hinduism, or an eclectic blend---it's all part of the soil" (qtd. in Oakland, op. cit. 14).

In this hotbed of deception in Graceland, one frequently needs to do a reality check. What began as a look at the emerging church has followed the "pebbled trail" all the way to the root of the New Age Movement. This became an unexpected pathway to follow in searching for truth regarding the emerging church. Incidentally, what was once referred to as New Age Spirituality has been renamed just New Spiritually.

Readers will find this book heavily documented in order for them to read for themselves the words and hear the hearts of the writers. This study has been enlightening, intriguing, challenging, and a bit scary at times. However, we must forge ahead and strive to follow the example of the sons of Issachar: "...of the children of Issachar, who had understanding of the times, to know what Israel ought to do ..." (1 Chronicles 12:32a).

One will find most chapters are written in the format of a "blog." This was done so that readers could hear dialogue of characters, sensing the emotions at each turn, as discoveries are made regarding the text. This will give readers time to take in the depth of information and enjoy the responses of characters along the way. The five characters in our blog are:

> **Brother Carviss** - a man of many years and uncountable hours studying God's Word. Brother Carviss will introduce the topics for each blog session, and he will be an anchor for the "blog-versation."
>
> **Laurie** - a retired educator who loves to do research.
>
> **Hannah** - a college student who is reading a book, *Castles in the Sand*. She is finding that the plot and events are sounding too familiar as she reflects on her own spiritual formation classes at school, as well as our blog discussions.
>
> **Hector** - an intellectual agnostic, who frequently comes down on the side of skepticism.
>
> **Will** - the fisherman and retired naval officer, who frequently has practical insight as wide as the sea.

CONTENTS

	Preface	iv
	Introduction	vi
1	Deception in Graceland	1
2	Absolute Truth Or A Reasonable Faith?	9
3	New Missiology	26
4	It's All About The Journey	41
5	The Gentle Lion: Heaven and Hell	58
6	The New Global Kingdom of God	71
7	New Revelation And New Spirituality	86
8	To Meditate Or Not To Meditate	99
9	Interfaith Marches On	115
10	Where Is This Going? Will The Real Church Please Stand Up?	128
11	Where Do We Go From Here?	140

<u>Appendices</u>

Chapter Questions For Reflection	151
Works Cited	156

@chapter_one

DECEPTION IN GRACELAND

> "There is a way that seems right to a man, but its end is the way of death."   (Proverbs 14:12)

Two children and six years later, he says he doesn't love her...and in fact he never did.

Now, that's deception!

The church board asked their secretary to do an intricate credit/debit trail, knowing they would fire her once their request was complete.

Now, that's deception!

She arranged double dates with her husband's boss, only to take off with him to live in Paris.

Now that's deception!

When a contradiction is observed in the pastor's life, he just says he believes both things equally.

Now, that's deception!

Eating small bites of cookies for hours means I'm just munching a little.

Now, that's deception!

The devil charades as Jesus Christ, and Christians follow him.

Now, that's deception!

Some lies are so far from the obvious truth, that deception is extremely short-lived. For example, a child promises she has not been in the cookie jar, although the yellow and pink icing is dripping from her chin like a puppy drooling for a Happy Hugs Biscuit! Bona fide deception, however, is so close to the truth, that only those alive to Father God's discernment will see it.

For readers who must see the last chapter first, here is a snippet from the final chapter. John MacArthur, in his book, *The Truth War*, cautions:

> So apostasy is a fact of all history, and there is never any kind of armistice in the Truth War. Our generation is certainly no exception to that rule. Some of the greatest threats to truth today come from within the visible church. Apostates are there in vast abundance---teaching lies, popularizing gross falsehoods, reinventing essential doctrines, and even redefining truth itself. They seem to be everywhere in the evangelical culture today, making merchandise of the gospel (MacArthur, Truth 72).

The emerging/emergent church appears to be the last, best vessel for navigating this paradigm shift into the high seas of the 21st Century Church. Joining with the interfaith movement, as evidenced by changing the story of God (of Christ), the emergent church reflects our postmodern culture of relativism, which leans on no absolute truth. Even so, this is difficult to comprehend when Christians for centuries have steadily based belief on the infallible Word of God. Many emergent communities think of life without absolutes (for example, the exclusiveness of the Word of God), so it is impossible to argue or agree. Furthermore, there is a serious lack of belief in absolute standards, and so we experience "deception in Graceland." We dare not take our Father's grace for granted and treat His ultimate plan of grace as defective. "For by grace you have been saved through faith, and that not of yourselves; it is the gift of God…" (Ephesians 2:8).

Since Christianity has become broad and all-embracing today, many people think there are no false teachers or apostates in the church. Further, they see no reason to battle for the truth since truth is paraded today as a concept that is infinitely pliable and ready to make room for all views. Incredibly, some people in the church even believe that truth is broad enough to take in all well-intentioned notions from non-Christian religions. This makes discernment and confrontation of apostasy especially difficult in our radically tolerant culture of today's postmodernism (MacArthur, Truth, op.cit. 72).

As we search further, we discover that the "new reformation," with its appealing manner in the emergent church, has deep roots within the New Age/New Spirituality movement. Warren Smith, in, *False Christ Coming. Does Anybody Care?* describes the deception that kept him and his wife involved in the New Age Movement for many years. Smith uses direct quotations, as do we, to explain:

> For some time now, my spiritual teachings had convinced me that I was a sinless, guiltless, perfect Son of God and that I was every bit as much a part of the universal Christ as Jesus or Buddha or anyone else. I had been taught that I was a holy part of God, inherently equal to Christ and that I didn't need to be saved, redeemed, or born again. Because evil was only an illusion, there was no evil to be saved from. I had believed that I was responsible for myself and my world and I was the creator of my own reality (Smith, False 59).

> We had put our faith in ourselves as God and not in God as God; by going within we had gone without. We had grossly underestimated our ability to not be deceived, and we had grossly overestimated the wisdom of our metaphysical teachers (Ibid. 61).

> When we could finally see through the spiritual deception, most of the Scriptures we had been reading clicked into place.

It was as if scales had fallen from our eyes, and suddenly the New Testament was flooded with light ... (Ibid. 61).

Some scriptures that spoke to the Smiths:

"I marvel that you are turning away so soon from Him who called you in the grace of Christ, to a different gospel, which is not another; but there are some who trouble you and want to pervert the gospel of Christ" (Galatians 1:6-7).

"Beware of false prophets, who come to you in sheep's clothing, but inwardly they are ravenous wolves" (Matthew 7:15).

"And Jesus answered and said to them: 'Take heed that no one deceives you. For many will come in My name, saying, "I am the Christ," and will deceive many'" (Matthew 24:4-5).

In 1965, Helen Schucman, a Columbia University Professsor of Medical Psychology, responded to an "inner voice" which told her that it wanted her to take notes on what would become *A Course In Miracles*. Later this "inner voice" identified itself as "Jesus" (Smith, False 17). According to Schucman's notes, this "Jesus" presented a whole new way of looking at the world, including a completely different gospel than the gospel found in the Bible. The New Age / New Gospel fully contradicted the Bible's Gospel of Jesus Christ. For example, *A Course in Miracles* taught that love is all there is; that we must know that fear, the opposite of love, is only an illusion; that this illusion, based on wrong thinking, must be corrected. The world must recognize that God, being love, is in everyone and everything, and that God is sinless, perfect, and "at one" with all creation. Therefore, all humanity, a part of God, is sinless, perfect, and needs no salvation. In fact, the only thing that stands in the way of man's attaining this peace for himself and his world is the "fear and separation" that some people imagine exists between them and God (Ibid. 18-19).

Warren Smith reveals that most of those who have read, studied, and believed in *A Course in Miracles* have never known or paid attention to the Bible's warnings of deceivers who would come bearing Christ's name and would actually pretend to be Him. In fact, the scriptural warnings are explicit that these false christs and false prophets will arise from within the church and seduce others with supernatural wonders and signs. At earlier times, it was hard to realize how these false teachers, with signs and wonders, would be able to convince even the most faithful believers in the true Christ that this New Spirituality was God's plan for "today."

"For false christs and false prophets will arise and show great signs and wonders, so as to deceive, if possible, even the elect" (Matthew 24:24).

Furthermore, as deceiving as it is for false christs to arise within our very selves or church family, *A Course in Miracles* is proof to all of us that these false "deities" are not always flesh and blood. Rather, they could also be lying spirits pretending to be a spirit guide, the Holy Spirit, our higher self, or even Jesus (Smith, False, op.cit. 63). The apostle Paul puts it this way: "Now the Spirit expressly says that in latter times some will depart from the faith, giving heed to deceiving spirits and doctrines of demons" (1 Timothy 4:1).

Again, Warren Smith explains:

> What we had thought to be spiritual truth had turned out to be nothing more than fiction. What we had believed to be the fiction of the Bible had ironically turned out to be the Gospel truth. The age of deception that had been predicted was already well on its way. In listening to our spiritual teacher, we had missed the many warnings that were being shouted to us from the pages of the Bible. We were, in reality, fallen human beings, prone to temptation, and easily overcome by evil. And although there was no way we could ever save ourselves, we could be saved by Jesus Christ – the true Son of God – whom God sent to set us free (Smith, False, op. cit. 65).

Therefore, the church needs to get its "Sea Legs," and go into prep as sailors on high, rough seas. This is no time for a dose of dimenhydrinate before going out on a little "Dolphin Watch." We must have rigorous SWAT training at every level of our being: physical, mental, and spiritual. Further, we must be adept at wearing the Full Armor of God, realizing specifically what each piece can accomplish in battle. Of highest importance is the ability to readily use the Shield of Faith (to quench the fiery darts of Satan), as well as the Sword of the Spirit (which is the Word of God). We must walk by faith, knowing that, "...without faith it is impossible to please Him, for he who comes to God must believe that He is, and that He is a rewarder of those who diligently seek Him" (Hebrews 11:6). The Sword of the Spirit is vital to success as we see in this verse, "My people are destroyed for lack of knowledge..." (Hosea 4:6a).

Equally important, the time of spiritual deception is heightened, evidenced by the "20 ft. waves" that continue to consume the land and barrel along the shoreline of mansions built on "30 ft. stilts." Homeowners are unbelievably calloused to the threat, defensive in their decision to carry on, unabated. Forecasts of tsunami-causing rumblings, in ear-splitting fortissimo, rage on the ocean floor but have no effect on the insensate inhabitants of the land. The message of the Word of God: "Therefore take up the whole armor of God, that you may be able to withstand in the evil day, and having done all, to stand" (Ephesians 6:13).

Max Lucado, in his book, *In the Eye of the Storm,* quotes a poignant illustration, "Authority." Frank Koch illustrates the importance of obeying the Laws of the Lighthouse.

> Two battleships assigned to the training squadron had been at sea on maneuvers in heavy weather for several days. I was serving on the lead battleship and was on watch on the bridge as night fell. The visibility was poor with patchy fog, so the

captain remained on the bridge keeping an eye on all activities.

Shortly after dark, the lookout on the wing reported,

"Light bearing on the starboard bow."

"Is it steady or moving astern?" the captain called out.

The lookout replied, "Steady, Captain," which meant we were on a dangerous collision course with that ship.

The captain then called to the signalman, "Signal that ship: 'We are on a collision course, advise you change course twenty degrees.'"

Back came the signal, "Advisable for you to change course twenty degrees."

The captain said, "Send: 'I'm a captain, change course twenty degrees.'"

"I'm a seaman second-class," came the reply. "You had better change course twenty degrees."

By that time the captain was furious. He spat out, "Send: 'I'm a battleship. Change course twenty degrees.'"

Back came the flashing light, "I'm a lighthouse."

"We changed course" (Lucado, 153).

Finally, let's not be so indifferent that we fail to pay attention to the guiding rudder of our own ship. Our guide, the Holy Spirit, gives crucial warnings from the Word of God. King Solomon admonished, "Let us hear the conclusion of the whole matter: 'Fear God and keep His commandments, for this is the whole duty of man. For God will bring every work into judgment, including every secret thing. Whether it is good or whether it is evil'" (Ecclesiastes 12:13-14).

Duped's fictional blog, which begins with Chapter two, was created and designed to observe discussion of present-day orthodoxy and orthopraxy in Christianity, both emergent and traditional. Later, the informational purposes of New Spirituality will be discussed. Next week's discussion will cover, "Absolute Truth Or Reasonable Faith?" Under this chapter heading, we'll be looking at two other topics: (1) Is it prudent to "just live like Jesus lived?" (2) Quantum Physics/Quantum Spirituality. Some books that you may want to reference are: Rob Bell's *Velvet Elvis*; Brian McLaren's *a Generous Orthodoxy;* DeYoung and Kluck's *Why We're Not Emergent;* Doug Pagitt's *A Christianity Worth Believing;* Roger Oakland's *Faith Undone;* Warren Smith's *A "Wonderful" Deception*; Leonard Sweet's *Quantum Spirituality*; John MacArthur's *The Truth War*; and Brian Greene's *The Fabric of the Cosmos*.

For those who would like to participate in the blog discussion, pro or con, please log in with your web chat name on Tuesday, August 9, at 8:00 p.m. Please have information and references available for discussion.

Until next week,

Meryl Carviss (blog host)

@chapter_two

ABSOLUTE TRUTH OR A REASONABLE FAITH?

> "Beware lest anyone cheat you through philosophy and empty deceit, according to the tradition of men, according to the basic principles of the world, and not according to Christ. For in Him dwells all the fullness of the Godhead bodily; and you are complete in Him, who is the head of all principality and power." (Colossians 2:8)

AUGUST 9, 2011 - STUDY FORUM BLOGGERS CHECKED IN:

>Brother Carviss >Laurie >Hannah "Campus-Joy" >Hector "Not-So-Fast" >Will "Square-Away"

<u>Brother Carviss</u> — 8:00 pm: Hello, fellow bloggers! We have a huge slice of information and understanding to cover, so let's get going! I'll open with a couple of quotations from John MacArthur's book, *The Truth War*.

> As always, a war is being waged against the truth. We are on one side or the other. There is no middle ground…no safe zone for the uncommitted. Lately the question of truth itself…what it is and whether we can truly know it at all…has become one of the major points of contention (MacArthur, Truth, op.cit. xxiii).

> If you were to challenge me to boil down postmodern thought into its pure essence and identify the gist of it in one single, simple, central characteristic, I would say it is the

rejection of every expression of certainty. In the postmodern perspective, certainty is regarded as inherently arrogant, elitist, intolerant, oppressive…and therefore always wrong (Ibid. 12).

<u>Not-So-Fast</u> – 8:08 pm: Wow, right out of the gate, you try to smash my stand – the middle ground. What's so wrong with playing it down the middle? Many people are just so eager to jump on one bandwagon or another, and then to condemn those who don't believe exactly as them. I'd rather just watch: it is really entertaining!

<u>Laurie</u> – 8:13 pm: Just keep watching, listening, and participating in this blog, Hector. One day you may have eyes to see it all differently. Now, I'd like to jump in with the issue of orthodoxy and orthopraxy. Actually, orthodoxy (belief) has to do with a soundness of doctrine, while orthopraxy (practice) reveals the action that orthodoxy requires. Notice DeYoung's conclusion of the practice of trying to live as closely to Jesus' way as possible, but without an understanding or response to the doctrine of Jesus' provision of salvation for all who will believe and accept Him as Savior.

Kevin DeYoung states,

> Besides being untrue, orthodoxy as orthopraxy is monumentally unhelpful. It sounds wonderful at first. Jesus is the best way to live. Where's the harm in that? After all, it is true that Jesus taught good ethics and set a good moral example. But if orthodoxy means I live the right way, the way of Jesus, I have no hope (DeYoung and Kluck 113).

<u>Brother Carviss</u> – 8:18 pm: A true concern regarding many emerging churches is that orthodoxy is second to orthopraxy. By this, I mean that right living, the Jesus way, is highlighted as the most important aspect of Christian living, leaving doctrinal issues (orthodoxy) to be identified and adhered to in small groups and communities of believers, ever changing as cultures evolve.

Further, DeYoung puts it this way:

> There are, however, more serious concerns with the emergent view of Jesus than just an overly realized, sometimes overly politicized kingdom message. Many emergent authors are very close to discarding, and some already have, historic understandings of the atonement, the existence of eternal punishment, and the uniqueness of Jesus Christ in salvation (Ibid. 192).

Many say, "Let's just live the way Jesus lived!" It's true that Jesus set the example of a pure life without sin, and yet our salvation is not dependent on how good of a job we do of following Jesus' way. As humans, we'll fail every time! It is by our admission of sin and our confession of faith in the death and resurrection of Jesus Christ (to pay our debt we could never pay) that we are saved, set free, and made able to live the way of Jesus!

Square-Away – 8:25 pm: I kind of got into Doug Pagitt's book, *A Christianity Worth Believing*. Now, he has some weird ideas, but he sure makes salvation for all people very inviting. I'm still chewing on his content! It seems to me that Doug is coming around it this way: Jesus' resurrection set all of creation into righteousness (right standing with God). It's (we're) already like that now, not ever having a specific time of asking for forgiveness, repenting, and asking Jesus into our hearts, thus being washed by the blood of Jesus. Therefore, we just hang out with Christ-followers and learn to live like Jesus by moving closer to God (Pagitt, Worth Believing 210-211).

Now, to a nautical guy like me, it seems that, in this way, there is never a point of "being saved," nor experiencing the miraculous touch that transforms a heart by the almighty love and power of God. There isn't that point of turning from death to life, from darkness to light, and from self-centeredness to God-centeredness. Doug Pagitt points out:

Jesus is saying that the way to God is to walk the path Jesus walked, the path of obedience, of integration, of partnership. That's why it matters that life and love won out. The point of the resurrection was to recalibrate the balance of creation, to bring all of it into sync with the agenda of God. The resurrection was God showing us, through Jesus, that living out the agenda of God means living out an agenda of love and life (Ibid. 210-211).

Campus-Joy – 8:33 pm: It's as if Jesus' death justified us and His resurrection gave us life, and furthermore set all things in creation aright, thus allowing people to turn from "disconnect" into "integration" with God, but without any power which is in salvation. The apostle Paul gave us a thorough description of humanity in the last days:

> But know this, that in the last days perilous times will come: for men will be lovers of themselves, lovers of money, boasters, proud, blasphemers, disobedient to parents, unthankful, unholy, unloving, unforgiving, slanderers, without self-control, brutal, despisers of good, traitors, headstrong, haughty, lovers of pleasure rather than lovers of God, having a form of godliness but denying its power. And from such people turn away (2 Timothy 3:1-5).

Square-Away – 8:42 pm: The sailor in me would call for the boatswain pipe to draw penetrating attention to this warning Paul gave to Timothy, especially in light of the following word game meant to lead us to be "co-creators" with God.

> Salvation, rescue, release, healing---they come through the God who created all things, the God who is alive and involved in all things, the God who is actively remaking all things. They come when we participate in a living, dynamic relationship with God and one another, here, now, and forevermore. ... It's created a framework in which all these

ideas about holism, the integrated God, and humanity as co-creators with God flow into a glorious worldview of hope and promise and possibility (Pagitt, Christianity, op.cit. 232-233).

Laurie – 8:48 pm: I personally have a difficult time recognizing this plan of salvation in which Jesus' resurrection recalibrated the balance of creation and brought all into sync with the agenda of God. Strangely, it sounds as if all people are universally saved and made right with God without any choice on their part. This perspective comes into clearer focus, however, when reading a quote from Barbara Marx Hubbard in her book, *Revelation*:

> Here we are, now poised either on the brink of destruction greater than the world has ever seen---a destruction which will cripple planet Earth forever and release only the few to go on---or on the threshold of global co-creation wherein each person on Earth will be attracted to participate in his or her own evolution to godliness (qtd. in Oakland 159).

This idea of "evolution to godliness" lends itself to the notion of "collective salvation." It is also akin to the mission of just getting closer and closer to God as we journey with other Christ-followers.

Not-So-Fast – 8:52 pm: I got into Kevin DeYoung and Ted Kluck's book, *Why We're Not Emergent (By Two Guys Who Should Be)*. Now that Ted guy almost speaks my language! Here's what he had to say about truth:

> ...As a Christian man, specifically a husband and father, I need truth. I need to worship a God who makes demands on my character, with consequences. I need to know that Christianity is about more than me just 'reaching my untapped potential' or 'finding the God inside me.' I need to know that I worship a Christ who died, bodily, and rose from the dead. Literally, I need to know that decisions can [and should] be made based on Scripture and not just experience.

> These are things that give me peace in a world of maybe (DeYoung and Kluck, op.cit. 28).

I also liked what Tony Jones, former national director of Emergent Village, had to say about truth when he explained that truth is a journey, not a destination. He also explained that emergent isn't a new name brand of Christianity. He said it's a way of thinking. Here's Ted Kluck's take on Jones' comments:

> Jones says that we're here not to determine absolute truth, but we're in a quest for a "reasonable faith." Reasonable according to whom, and whether what is reasonable for me will be reasonable for Moby, Jones, Africa, Bono, or anyone else, he doesn't say. And whether that same faith will be reasonable for me at age fifty, he doesn't say either (Ibid. 227).

Kevin DeYoung shares about *absolute* versus *relevant*, as he quotes Barry Taylor in Doug Pagitt's *Emergent Manifesto*.

> "Whether 'Christianity' has any future at all as a vibrant expression of faith in the Man from Galilee is a matter of debate as far as I am concerned," writes Taylor. "Perhaps the times call for something else, something other, not merely the repackaging of old metaphors (playing the 'relevant' game) but a new incarnation of what it means to follow Jesus" (qtd. in DeYoung and Kluck, op.cit. 115).

Now this last one is a little over my spiritual head, but this Barry dude has the aura of the rebel I see in myself. So, I think I like him!

<u>Square-Away</u> – 9:14 pm: Aye, Aye, Hector! I sense the waft of a soul adrift here. Let's just belay judgment on these comments and take a drink from the Word of God:

"My son, fear the Lord and the king: do not associate with those given to change" (Proverbs 24:21).

"Jesus Christ is the same yesterday, today, and forever" (Hebrews 13:8).

"For I am the Lord, I do not change..." (Malachi 3:6).

> Behold, the days are coming," says the Lord God, "that I will send a famine on the land, not a famine of bread, nor a thirst for water, but of hearing the words of the Lord. They shall wander from sea to sea, and from north to east; they shall run to and fro, seeking the word of the Lord, but shall not find it (Amos 8:11-12).

<u>Not-So-Fast</u> – 9:20 pm: OK, Captain Square-Away! I can see the contrast in these two points of view. If I only believed that the Bible was God's Word, that God was even real, then I might take notice. Actually, I see myself as an agnostic: one who believes that a man should not say he knows or believes that for which there is no proof. I see the question of God's existence as impossible to answer, that proof for or against is not reliable. So I've made my decision to stay with what I know in the natural realm. Some say this is a type of spiritualism called Pantheism. If Pantheism spells out a deep reverence for belonging with nature and protecting it, as well as deep concern for social justice, then I am a Pantheist agnostic, I suppose. They say the only question I need ask myself is, "Does it feel right to me to reverence, or worship, nature with all its living components?" I'd give a rousing "Amen" to that question!

<u>Laurie</u> – 9:25 pm: Hector, keep searching for the truth in God's Word! You'll find His truth in time! Moving to another author, did anyone else read Rob Bell? I think I may have grasped his message by now. Rob Bell, in his *Velvet Elvis*, sets a foundation for why questioning God is a good thing. He, in fact, says that questioning God is central to our Christian experience, freeing us from having to have it all figured out, freeing us from feeling like we need to have answers to everything (Bell, Velvet 31).

Now, surely there are times when we don't understand the events in this life, or when we have too few facts to make an illumined assessment about a decision. On the other hand, however, we are admonished to "...sanctify the Lord God in your hearts, and always be ready to give a defense to everyone who asks you a reason for the hope that is in you, with meekness and fear..." (1 Peter 3:15).

Further in Bell's *Velvet Elvis*, we follow his reasoning on questioning God until he concludes that the mystery *is* actually the truth (Bell, Velvet, op.cit. 33). Going on, Bell reaches by saying, "It's not so much that the Christian faith *has* a lot of paradoxes. It's that it *is* a lot of paradoxes. And we can't resolve a paradox. We have to let it be what it is" (Ibid. 34).

Next, we are invited by Rob Bell to jump on the trampoline of life (with springs being the metaphor for beliefs). Bell says, "You don't have to know anything about the springs to pursue living 'the way'" (Ibid.).

We don't need to understand anything about belief in order to pursue living the way Jesus lived? Talk about blind faith! Look at the apostle Paul's encouragement to young Timothy:

> I charge you therefore before God and the Lord Jesus Christ, who will judge the living and the dead at His appearing and His kingdom: preach the word! Be ready in season and out of season. Convince, rebuke, exhort, with all longsuffering and teaching. For the time will come when they will not endure sound doctrine, but according to their own desires, because they have itching ears, they will heap up for themselves teachers; and they will turn their ears away from the truth, and be turned aside to fables (II Timothy 4:1-4).

Rob Bell continues with, "I want to invite people to actually live this way so the life Jesus offers gradually becomes their life. It becomes less and less about talking, and more and more about the experience we are actually having" (Bell, Velvet, op.cit. 35).

This makes me think of an analogy: I could be with people who know a lot about Mother Theresa. I could try to walk in generosity and selfless love as I hear these people talk about her. However, I would never come close to living "the way" of Mother Theresa unless I miraculously took on her nature. This is precisely what Jesus' atonement did for us: the miracle of humans being "born again" to do the works of Jesus because we are wearing His nature (His glory, His righteousness) and empowered by His Spirit. Without this miraculous atonement for our sinful nature, we remain "nothing."

Jesus explains, "I am the vine; you are the branches. He who abides in me and I in him, bears much fruit; for without me you can do nothing" (John 15:5). And, a stern warning from Jesus, "If anyone does not abide in me he is thrown away like a branch and withers; and the branches are gathered, thrown into the fire, and burned" (John 15:6).

<u>Brother Carviss</u> – 9:43 pm: Now, we'll apply the spiritual hypothesis of "a reasonable faith outshines absolute truth" to the world of a science of probability. In the final part of this chapter, we will delve into a current phenomenon known as quantum mechanics, specifically quantum physics. When we are admonished to just live as Jesus lived, think like Jesus thought, and be interconnected with the Cosmos as Jesus was, we must realize that these terms radiate a totally new futuristic kind of philosophy.

In a nutshell, quantum mechanics (quantum physics) proposes that we can now identify particles smaller than the atom, and some of these particles can travel faster than the speed of light. It follows that this new knowledge, much of which is explained in Brian Greene's book, *The Fabric of the Cosmos*, leads the reader to accept that these new scientific discoveries change much of what we "know" about space and time. Actually, the development of these theories dovetails to support the New Spirituality's premise that humanity must discard what we have believed to be true and accept the hypothesis that we are in a new wave rushing to crash onto the shore of a different paradigm. These quantum particles are unpredictable, not always acting the same at different times or in various places. It seems somehow that the particles respond to the observer and the observer's desires. Now a bridge has been actualized from physics to spirituality. As an extension of this concept, we have a "quantum spirituality," as presented by emerging church leader, Dr. Leonard Sweet.

Bottom Line: new discoveries can render null and void some scientific laws we have treated as truth. These discoveries are credited as bringing forth a knowledge that God is in all things, including all humanity. Therefore, all humanity is "God," and a part of the universal body of "Christ," whether each person knows it or not. This leads to the belief that all humanity is expected to accept the New Spirituality's premise that we must move in "oneness and love." Those who do not choose to follow this belief, but rather remain faithful to the Bible's Jesus Christ as the only way to salvation, will suffer because they will be accused of following an illusion of "separation and fear." Further, since all time and space is supposedly not as we had thought, many miracles are now scientifically explained using the new paradigm of "spacetime" (Smith, Wonderful 173-174). This perverted gospel will be treated more fully in a later blogging session.

<u>Campus-Joy</u> - 10:00 pm: I'd like to add to the phenomenon of quantum physics by referencing chapter four of Brian Green's book: *The Fabric Of The Cosmos*. We've been plowing through his work on "entangling space" in my college science class. While Einstein's work in relativity shifted Newton's theories about the universe, a new scientific revolution crept in at the beginning of the 20th Century. Intense study continued for three decades, until the 1930's, when a new and unconventional formulation was brought forth: "quantum mechanics" (B. Greene, Fabric, op.cit. 78).

Recognizing that the theory of relativity used extremes of gravity and speed to show its effects, we now realize that quantum mechanics reveals itself in another extreme situation: the reality of the extremely tiny. Another difference in these two theories is that relativity uses comparison to explain a view of reality, while quantum mechanics does not need to use comparison. It appears more difficult to train one's mind to have quantum mechanical intuition, since quantum mechanics destroys one's own personal conception of reality (Ibid.).

What fascinates me is that, according to *The Fabric of the Cosmos*, quantum mechanics works with particles smaller than atoms, so we cannot ever know the specific location and exact velocity of even one particle. This makes it impossible to predict with total certainty the outcome of even the simplest experiment, let alone the evolution of the whole cosmos. The best physicists can do with quantum mechanics is to predict a probable hypothesis, but through decades of incredibly accurate experiments, physicists can now say that neither the Newtonian nor the Einsteinian metaphors are tenable. Therefore, it is believed that these past theories are demonstrably *not* how the world works (Ibid. 79).

Brother Carviss – 10:15 pm: To explore this even further, physicists have long recognized a feature of the universe known as *locality*. Locality emphasizes the idea that one can physically, directly affect only things that are in close proximity (or local). Experiments with quantum physics, however, strongly support the conclusion that the universe, as we know it, admits interconnections which are not local (Ibid. 80).

Brian Greene explains:

> Something that happens over here can be entwined with something that happens over there even if nothing travels from here to there – and even if there isn't enough time for anything, even light, to travel between the events. This means that space cannot be thought of as it once was: intervening space, regardless of how much there is, does not ensure that

two objects are separate, since quantum mechanics allow an entanglement, a kind of connection, to exist between them. A particle, like one of the countless number that make up you or me, can run but it can't hide (Ibid. 80-81).

According to quantum theory and the many experiments that bear out its predictions, the quantum connection between two particles can persist even if they are on opposite sides of the universe. From the standpoint of their entanglement, notwithstanding the many trillions of miles of space between them, it's as if they are right on top of each other. Numerous assaults on our conception of reality are emerging from modern physics . . . but of those that have been experimentally verified, I find none more mind-boggling than the recent realization that our universe is not local (Ibid. 80-81).

<u>Not-So-Fast</u> – 10:21 pm: There it is: even the theories and laws of science are not firm! With this quantum breakthrough, we have to admit that things are not always as they seem, that there is always the probability that we need to revise our many hypotheses applied to the natural and supernatural worlds. This is precisely why I remain an agnostic!

<u>Square-Away</u> – 10:23 pm: Particles smaller than an atom, traveling faster than the speed of light, entwined with particles trillions of miles away, thus "explaining" miracles of the Bible and of current times...! Wow, Hector, that makes my head spin, too, but somehow it seems to me that the connection between "quantum physics" and "quantum spiritually" appears all too easy to make!

<u>Laurie</u> – 10:28 pm: It seems that some thoughts from Warren Smith's book, *A "Wonderful" Deception*, may be just what we need right now. Warren Smith intimates that many with mystic and New Age connections are teaching that God is "in" every atom, and so it follows that God is "in" everything, including humanity. According to these

teachers, if follows that we are all "One," and, since God is in all, then all are "God." On the contrary, even though humans share one blood (physically through Adam and Eve), there is no spiritual oneness. The apostle Paul made this clear when, after telling the Greeks they shared one blood, Acts 17:26, he let them know that the only spiritual oneness was in Jesus Christ and in His blood shed on Calvary (Smith, Wonderful, op. cit. 43). "For you are all sons of God through faith in Christ Jesus. For as many of you as were baptized into Christ have put on Christ. There is neither Jew nor Greek, there is neither slave nor free, there is neither male nor female; for you are all one in Christ Jesus" (Galatians 3:26-28).

Being one in Christ Jesus does not represent a given universal oneness. Paul is explicit that Christ Jesus died for our sins, and it's only when we repent, then accept Him as our Savior that we are saved and set free from our sin. "…for all have sinned, and fall short of the glory of God, being justified freely by His grace through the redemption that is in Christ Jesus…" (Romans 3:23-24). Paul exhorts the young minister, "O Timothy! Guard what was committed to your trust, avoiding the profane and vain babblings and contradictions of what is falsely called knowledge [science] – by professing it, some have strayed concerning the faith…" (1 Timothy 6:20-21). It seems that Paul, in expecting things like quantum physics and quantum spirituality, is warning Timothy that a time would come when people would follow false teachers who would turn them away from the one and only true, living God. In the same light, Paul is also warning Timothy to avoid being spiritually compromised by pseudo-scientific teaching (Smith, Wonderful, op.cit. 148-149).

Brother Carviss – 10:41 pm: The all important nugget here is to realize that New Spirituality's worldview proclaims that "chaos" can be overcome when all of humanity acknowledges that it is not "separate," but rather sees itself as "One" – a part of the "God" that is "in" everybody and everything. A careful look at God's Word will show that humanity is not "God" or "One" with God (John 2:24-25). The Bible teaches just the opposite – that man is actually separated from God by sin (Isaiah 59:2). It is because of this 'separation' that we need to acknowledge our sin and repent (Acts 2: 38). Everyone must be born again ... (John 3:6-7). The narrow and only way to eternal salvation is in repenting and accepting Christ Jesus as our Lord and Savior (Smith, Wonderful, op. cit. 144-145).

It seems we are expected to believe that all creation is an interconnected quantum field of energy and oneness (that is "God"). New Spirituality leaders tell us humanity will survive and have a positive future only if we all accept and play our role, as "God" in this interconnected quantum "Field of Dreams" (Ibid. 154).

Campus-Joy – 10:52 pm: *What the Bleep Do We Know!?* is a 2004 movie completely devoted to the topic of quantum physics. This DVD draws viewers to New Spirituality/New Worldview concepts. Ph.D. physicists and other experts are teamed with occult channeler, J.Z. Knight in order to use quantum physics to infer that we are all "one" because God is "in" everything. The movie attempts to communicate that all of creation is interconnected at a sub-atomic level. There is also the assertion that the principles of quantum physics will help all people create a reality of their own (Ibid. 172).

Not-So-Fast – 10:57 pm: What's so bad about that? I'm all for being in control of my own life, my own reality.

Campus-Joy – 10:59 pm: The claim is made that an inner peace can be achieved as synapses in our brains are reprogrammed, by us, to not occur in response to personal addictions, such as resentment, anger, envy, or even promiscuous ties. In this way, we can create our own realities.

> By making the speculative "quantum leap" from physics to metaphysics, *What the Bleep Do We Know!?* argues that as humanity comes to recognize that '"we are all one" because God is "in" everything, then mankind – collectively as "God"

– can and will create a positive, peaceful future. In the movie, New Age channeler J.Z. Knight channels an allegedly ancient spirit named "Ramtha." This familiar spirit proceeds to provide what seems to be spiritual corroboration for the "experts" in the movie. In an attempt to unite science and the New Age in an irrefutable quantum way, the channeled Ramtha makes this comment: "We have the epitome of a great science…quantum physics…Everyone is God" (Qtd. in Smith, Wonderful 172-173).

Square-Away – 11:05 pm: Finally, we're getting the connection between this bizarre "science" and a new mysterious "faith." Hector, are you getting this?

Not-So-Fast – 11:08 pm: Oh, sure, don't you? Actually, I don't know why exactly I keep going with this blog. I don't even believe in God. Why would I even follow all this technical stuff applied to faith?

Campus-Joy – 11:11 pm: Emerging church leader, Dr. Leonard Sweet, in his book, *Quantum Spirituality*, has expressed links between the global church of the 21st Century and an altered state of consciousness, sometimes referred to as the Christ consciousness:

> The church is fundamentally one being, one person, a communion whose cells are connected to one another within the information network called the Christ consciousness (Sweet, Quantum 122).

> Energy-fire experiences take us into ourselves only that we might reach outside of ourselves. Metanoia is a de-centering experience of connected-ness and community. It is not an exercise in reciting what Jesus has done for me lately. Energy-fire ecstasy, more a buzz than a binge, takes us out of ourselves, literally. That is the meaning of the word "ecstatic'" (Ibid. 93).

> The power of small groups is in their ability to develop the discipline to get people "in-phase" with the "Christ consciousness" and connected with one another (Ibid. 147).
>
> New Lights offer up themselves as the cosmion incarnating the cells of a new body. New Lights will function as transitional vessels through which transforming energy can renew the divine image in the world, moving postmoderns from one state of embodiment to another (Ibid. 48).
>
> A surprisingly central feature of all the world's religions is the language of light in communicating the divine and symbolizing the union of the human with the divine: Muhammed's light-filled cave, Moses' burning bush, Paul's blinding light, Fox's "inner light," Krishna's Lord of Light, Bohme's light-filled cobbler ship. Plotinus' fire experiences, Bodhisattvas with the flow of Kundalini's fire (Ibid. 235).

<u>Laurie</u> – 11:21 pm: Well, I'll have to say that this emergent church leader sheds a "floodlight" on the understanding of quantum spirituality. There's not much room for confusion in Dr. Sweet's explanation. Now, let's look at this note of summation from Warren B. Smith in *A "Wonderful" Deception*, p. 174:

> The new worldview of the New Age/New Spirituality argues that for the good of the world and for a positive peaceful future, humanity must come to recognize that we are all "one" because we are all "part" of the quantum field or "System" that is God. By seeing yourself as part of God – "the System" – you will ultimately save yourself and save the world. This is the New Paradigm. This is the New Age/New Spirituality described by quantum physics. This is the new emerging worldview. And this is the lie. It is the serpent in the Garden of Eden all over again.

Brother Carviss – 11:26 pm: I can't think of any better comment with which to end this session! I'm learning from all of you. I hope that you also can say that! Next week, our topic will be "The New Missiology." Some books that you may want to reference are: Brian McLaren's *a Generous Orthodoxy;* DeYoung and Kluck's *Why We're Not Emergent;* Erwin McManus' *The Barbarian Way;* Roger Oakland's *Faith Undone;* Brian McLaren's *The Secret Message of Jesus;* John MacArthur's *The Truth War.*

Until next week, August 16th at 8:00,

Meryl Carviss (blog host)

@chapter_three

NEW MISSIOLOGY

"Why is it so vital to fight for the truth?"

"Because truth is the only thing that can liberate people from the bondage of sin and give them eternal life."

(John MacArthur)

AUGUST 16, 2011 - STUDY FORUM BLOGGERS CHECKED IN:

>Brother Carviss >Laurie >Hannah "Campus-Joy" >Hector "Not-So-Fast" >Will "Square-Away"

Brother Carviss — 8:00 pm: Hi bloggers, are you ready to begin? We have several authors to reference tonight, so I'll lay a little groundwork on a new missiology. There appears to be a change in meaning from traditional "missionary work" to the new missiology. The traditional view of Christian mission work entails Christians going into various cultures in order to bring the saving Gospel of Jesus Christ to people who have not had the opportunity to hear and believe that gospel. On the other hand, the new missiology of the emerging church seeks to reach people in diverse cultures with a new way: the "way of Jesus."

Brian McLaren demonstrates a blending of world faiths by explaining that he doesn't believe making disciples necessarily means pointing new believers to the Christian religion. Further, McLaren points out that, in many circumstances, it may be helpful for new believers in Jesus to just stay within their current world religious settings. In this framework, people who become followers of Jesus will simply be known as Hindu followers of Jesus, Buddhist followers of Jesus, etc. (McLaren, Generous 293, 297).

This commentary makes me think of the prophet Amos' words, "Can two walk together unless they are agreed?" (Amos 3:3).

Paul the Apostle instructs:

> Let no one deceive you with empty words, for because of these things the wrath of God comes upon the sons of disobedience. Therefore do not be partakers with them. For you were once darkness, but now you are light in the Lord. Walk as children of light (for the fruit of the Spirit is in all goodness, righteousness, and truth), proving what is acceptable to the Lord. And have no fellowship with the unfruitful works of darkness, but rather expose them (Ephesians 5:6-11).

Campus Joy – 8:27 pm: This McLaren information sounds a lot like a book I've been reading by Erwin McManus, *The Barbarian Way*. Mr. McManus states that Christianity is seen as just another world religion, and that all world religions should be about promoting the Jesus revolution began 2000 years ago (McManus, 9).

Laurie – 8:30 pm: Hi everyone! I found a little synopsis of three things the new missiology says:

> 1. You can keep your own religion — Buddhism, Islam, Hinduism … you just need to add Jesus to the equation. Then you become complete. You become a Buddhist with Jesus, a Hindu with Jesus, a Muslim with Jesus and so on.
>
> 2. You can throw out the term Christianity and still be a follower of Jesus.

3. In fact, you can throw out the term Christian too. In some countries you could be persecuted for calling yourself a Christian, and there is no need for that. Just ask Jesus into your heart, you don't have to identify yourself as a Christian (New Missiology On-Line).

<u>Not-So-Fast</u> – 8:43 pm: You know, this sounds like a wonderfully peaceful solution to all the fighting people do over religion. If each sect weren't so self absorbed in thinking their way was the only right way to God, the world's people might just learn how to find common ground and accept each other's beliefs as all leading to the same religious place. I mean, I don't believe in any of this religious stuff, but the whole world would be a happier place if all the religious fighting stopped!

<u>Campus-Joy</u> – 8:47 pm: During the week, I read a lot of Roger Oakland's *Faith Undone*. He cautions:

> My concern lies with the way missions is changing and how the Gospel is being presented. To say that someone does not have to leave their pagan religion behind, and in fact they don't have to even stop calling themselves Hindu or Muslim, is not presenting the teachings of the Bible (Oakland, op. cit. 177).

Interestingly, the apostle Paul, who would later give up his life for faith in Christ, was clear when exhorting Christians in Philippi: "But indeed I also count all things loss for the excellence of the knowledge of Christ Jesus my Lord, for whom I have suffered the loss of all things, and count them as rubbish that I may gain Christ" (Philippians 3:8).

Hector, if you'd open your heart just a tiny bit, you just might be pleasantly surprised at what Father God would show you. I'm only encouraging you, not putting you down.

Square-Away – 8:55 pm: Aye, aye, Mates, I've waited for many a bumboat, which lay at the ship's booms peddling their wares and supplies. However, I've never been sold a bill of goods that could compare to the bilge of this new missiology! In fact, I'm appreciating my precious time at sea and fishing as a continual breath of fresh air, when contrasted with this "genius-level Anchor-Canker." This week I've enjoyed reading DeYoung and Kluck's book, *Why We're Not Emergent*. I actually waded through some holistic debris touted by a mover and a shaker of the emergent church, Spencer Burke. A prominent voice in emergent conversation, Burke is the creator of theooze.com and the host of Soularize, a semi-annual postmodern/emergent conference. (Both theooze.com and Soularize will close out late in 2011, to enter new phases of transformatioin.) Kevin DeYoung refers to Spencer Burke's philosophy of doctrine, or lack thereof, when he states that Burke has little (no?) place for doctrinal belief.

According to Burke:

> What you believe about Jesus or the work He accomplished is irrelevant. Jesus' vision of God is "for anyone and everyone, Jewish, Christian, Buddhist, whatever …..What counts is not a belief system but a holistic approach of following what you feel, experience, discover, and believe; it is a willingness to join Jesus in his vision for a transformed humanity" (qtd. in DeYoung and Kluck , op. cit. 120).

DeYoung goes on to say that Burke's idea of the Christian life is absolutely devoid of the Gospel of Jesus Christ's life, death, resurrection, ascension, exaltation, and coming again. Burke's conception of discipleship is seen as parallel to any ordinary self-help guru (Ibid. 121).

Brother Carviss – 9:05 pm: Exactly what is the goal of this neo-world religious movement? Some believe we are morphing into a new era of Christianity, one that will be a true global community. When this happens, it is thought that there will, of necessity, be a convergence of thought and experience which will lead to a relationship we have never before known.

Why does this make me think of the Tower of Babel? The plan of men in Genesis 11, was to build themselves a city and a tower whose top is in the heavens. They wanted to make a name for themselves, and be in such union that they would not be scattered across the earth. God, of course, seeing the pride of their purpose, confused their language into many tongues, and indeed did scatter them throughout the face of all the earth.

Just so, in the end, I believe God will allow man enough time to make his evil plans and to carry them out. I believe there will be a global world religion, and a false peace until the time is right for God to powerfully carry out His plan for the end of this age. Jesus clearly tells us, "Take heed that no man deceive you. For many shall come in my name, saying, 'I am Christ;' and shall deceive many" (Matthew 24: 4-5).

<u>Laurie</u> – 9:15 pm: As we have seen, many believe that we can all accept Jesus as part of our belief system. For deception to be deceiving, it must follow the truth very closely, with just a sleight of hand twist to accomplish its own destructive outcome. I've been thinking about the pathway of multicultural inclusion, or relativity of belief. Following are four tenets of multicultural inclusion, as I see it:

1. Each culture has its own way of knowing God and is equally acceptable: i.e. Islam, Jewish, Christianity, Hinduism, Buddhism, etc.
2. Within Postmodern Christianity, there is also cultural contextualization, meaning that theology (the study of God) is an ever-changing understanding of who God is, based on the particular cultural setting upon which one rests.

3. Relativity says, "Come on in. Let's journey together with the goal of getting closer to God, believing there is no absolute way to God."
4. Even within any given culture at any particular time, there may be many different views, or "conversations," going on simultaneously.

I've been reading Brian McLaren's *The Secret Message of Jesus*. McLaren is a rather subtle writer, so I've had to really think about what I'm reading. In *The Secret Message of Jesus*, McLaren describes a co-creating of religious unity. When striving for that unity, it is vital to discern some common areas of cultural appreciation. For example, when considering Jesus, Muslims regard Him as a great prophet, Hindus will consider Him as one manifestation of divinity, and Buddhists see Him as a most enlightened person. McLaren maintains that if we can come together on aspects which are commonly acceptable with each religion, then we are perhaps looking at some meaningful dialogue (McLaren, Secret, op. cit. 7).

Square-Away – 9:24 pm: McLaren's idea of a secret message makes me think of the ancient/future notion of Gnosticism. Even as emerging churches make it well understood that they do not all espouse to the same set of beliefs, Gnostic thinking offered many designs of sects, each developed by its own community. Because of this, Gnosticism was, and remains, a difficult system to describe and refute. John MacArthur explains:

> Every form of Gnosticism starts with the notion that truth is a secret known only by a select few elevated, enlightened minds. (Hence the name, from gnosis, the Greek word for knowledge). Gnostics offered a sinister smorgasbord of ideas, myths, and superstitions, all borrowed from pagan mystery religions and human philosophy. Those beliefs were then blended with Christian imagery and terminology. When the gospel accounts of Jesus' teaching didn't fit Gnostic doctrines,

Gnostics simply wrote their own fictional "gospels" and passed them off as more enlightened accounts of Christ's life and ministry (MacArthur, Truth, op. cit. 89).

John MacArthur continues to lead us to understand the role of Gnosticism in postmodern culture. He explains when considering Gnosticism today, it is worth noting that Gnostics have a focused tendency to synthesize Christian symbolism and doctrine with their secular beliefs, thus deceiving many Christians. After borrowing biblical terminology, redefining terms, and revamping Christian teaching, Gnostics then appear as Christians who are more enlightened than most. Gnostics frequently align themselves with established churches in order to gain credibility (Ibid. 90).

Not-So-Fast – 9:30 pm: Oh yes, just follow religious programming on cable TV, and you'll get a full course meal of "Who's Who in Advanced Enlightenment!"

Laurie – 9:32 pm: Back to *The Secret Message of Jesus*, McLaren also puts out the questions: "What if Jesus' secret message reveals a secret plan? What if he didn't come to start a new religion, but rather came to start a political, social, religious, artistic, economic, intellectual, and spiritual revolution that would give birth to a new world" (McLaren, Secret, op. cit. 4)?

Some actually thought that was the plan when Jesus went about His ministry on Earth, demonstrating His power. Jesus quickly corrected that assessment when He told them that His Kingdom was not of this world. (John 18:36)

Brother Carviss – 9:35 pm: I found a nugget for thought in Berit Kjos' on-line article, "Who Defines the Kingdom of God?" Kjos asserts:

> Yet emerging church movements today are still trying to move the boundaries of His Kingdom. They have redefined God's Word and are fast embracing the latest versions of the old Gnostic quest for secret knowledge (gnosis) and self-

actualization, whether through mystical experience or collective imagination (Kjos).

Laurie – 9:43 pm: McLaren amplifies the notion that we should make it clear that the kingdom of God is open to all, except those who are not willing to accept its purposes. The postmodern culture strives for purposeful inclusion rather than exclusiveness and rejection, but it cannot include those who are opposed to its purpose (McLaren, Secret, op. cit. 167).

Square-Away – 9:47 pm: I kind of crossed over after reading Rob Bell's *Velvet Elvis*, and ventured into Rob Bell's book, *Sex God*. Shockingly, after reading *Sex God*, one may assume that God is not a holy God who is angered by sin, and who consequently sent His Son to die in our place so that divine justice may be satisfied. Rather, God shows Himself as a vulnerable lover who exposes Himself to rejection in order to be with us since we are so worth dying for (98, 112).

Kevin DeYoung responds to Bell's proposition:

> I have no doubt that this message will find a receptive audience, but it is not the message the apostles proclaimed and for which they died. Christians don't get killed for telling people that God believes in them and suffers like them and can heal their brokenness. They get killed for calling sinners to repentance and proclaiming faith in the crucified Son of God as the only means by which we who were enemies might be reconciled to God (Romans 5:10) (DeYoung and Kluck, op. cit. 195).

John MacArthur speaks to this postmodern attitude toward truth:

> …according to postmodernists, the subjectivity of the human mind makes knowledge of objective truth impossible. So it is useless to think of truth in objective terms. Objectivity is an illusion. Nothing is certain, and the thoughtful person will never speak with too much conviction about anything. Strong

convictions about any point of truth are judged supremely arrogant and hopelessly naïve. "Everyone is entitled to his own truth," according to postmodernists (MacArthur, Truth, op. cit. 11).

<u>Not-So-Fast</u> — 10:00 pm: I guess I'm a true postmodernist, because this freedom from conviction and exclusion speaks to my logic. I think lots of things are illusions, such as fear, joy, and even sin. Most people take this life much too seriously. Hey, we're here by chance, and our ups and downs are common to all men. Who really knows if we'll have chances to live other lives on this planet or at some other cosmic destination? Just cut all those cords, my friends, and breathe! Enjoy the ride! Who cares who thinks they are right or wrong? What are "right and wrong," but illusions?

<u>Brother Carviss</u> — 10:05 pm: Hopefully, Hector, as we continue our blog study, you'll begin to see these things differently. I'm proud of you for hanging in there with us! Now, let's bring it together by seeing that people from any and all world religions, through spiritual formation and contemplative prayer, take on a "Christ consciousness." This "Christ consciousness" would not lead them to leave their current religion. Rather, they just add on Jesus, and come closer to the united new spirituality which will be the hub around which the final apostate global church will turn.

<u>Campus Joy</u> — 10:08 pm: I have some thoughts from other authors, as discussed in Roger Oakland's *Faith Undone*. An article entitled "Christ-Followers in India Flourishing Outside the Church," by H. L. Richard, expands the idea that one doesn't have to become a Christian or to change his religious practices. Rather, he just needs to add Jesus to his spirituality:

> However, some might argue that this [the "smothering embrace of Hinduism"] is the danger with the *ishta devata* strategy I am proposing. It will lead not to an indigenous Christianity but to a Christianized Hinduism. Perhaps more

accurately we should say a Christ-ized Hinduism. I would suggest that really both are the same, and therefore we should not worry about it. We do not want to change the culture or the religious genius of India. We simply want to bring Christ and His Gospel into the center of it (qtd. in Oakland, op. cit. 176).

Herbert Hoefer, author of *Churchless Christianity*, has done extensive research regarding this "churchless" issue. He presents the proposition that rather than rejecting or changing the Muslim or Hindu culture, missionaries should just "Christ-ize" them. Hoefer shares that there are thousands of believers in India who he refers to as "non-baptized believers." This means that many who have been "Christ-ized" do not confess this openly because of fear of social or financial loss and status. Many do not even share with their friends or families to avoid ridicule and suspicion (Ibid. 176-177).

In *Idolatry in Their Hearts*, a book by Mike Oppenheimer and Sandy Simpson, they demonstrate how popular this new missiology has become. Following are some comments made by new missiology proponents as quoted in Roger Oakland's *Faith Undone*, pp. 178-179:

> "New Light embodiment means to be 'in connection' and 'information' with other faiths. One can be a faithful disciple of Jesus Christ without denying the flickers of the sacred in followers of Yahweh, Kali, or Krishna." –Leonard Sweet

> "I see no contradiction between Buddhism and Christianity. ... I intend to become as good a Buddhist as I can." – Thomas Merton

> "Allah is not another God. We worship the same God ... the same God! The very same God we worship in Christ is the God that the Jews ... and the Muslims ... worship." -Peter Kreeft

Oppenheimer and Simpson well document this paradigm shift in Christian missions. They explain:

> One cannot be in relationship with Jesus within the confines of a false religion. One must leave his or her religion to follow Jesus, not just add Him on .... This broadens Jesus' statement of the road being narrow into a wide, all encompassing concept. What is concerning is that these same kinds of statements are also made by those who are New Agers that hold a universal view. Alice Bailey [New Ager leader who coined the term New Age] said, "I would point out that when I use the phrase 'followers of the Christ' I refer to all those who love their fellowmen, irrespective of creed or religion" (qtd. in Oakland, op. cit. 179).

Square-Away – 10:25 pm: Apology is due to all the faithful Christian martyrs throughout the ages, and unto this present day, who have laid their allegiance and trust in Jesus Christ on the altars of ridicule, financial and family loss, as well as loss of their physical lives rather than to deny their Lord and Savior. Jesus says it best: "Whosoever therefore shall confess me before men, him will I confess also before my Father which is in heaven. But whosoever shall deny me before men, him will I also deny before my Father which is in heaven" (Matthew 10:32-33).

In addition, the apostle Peter instructs: "But sanctify the Lord God in your hearts, and always be ready to give a defense to everyone who asks you a reason for the hope that is in you, with meekness and fear" (I Peter 3:15).

Laurie – 10:30 pm: Some teach that the Gospel of the scripture is exclusive, promoting only one way to salvation: Jesus Christ received by grace through faith alone. On the other hand, some find an exponential inclusiveness with the New Spirituality of the "Kingdom Now" message. It would appear that the wall between biblical Christianity and pagan belief is disappearing, and that a new deceptive interfaith message is in the midst of us. Ironically, it seems apparent that a bridge is ready for use whereby all religious systems will be united in the name of the Christ, by eliminating the exclusiveness of the Gospel of Jesus Christ.

Square-Away – 10:33 pm: That statement, Laurie, tends to twist my brain like an eel entangled in seaweed! However, I see your point, and it seems that an ambiguity of language is used in this time to bring about confusion. MacArthur reminds us that many in our current culture would say that we should just set aside our differences about doctrine and devote our lives to showing the love of Christ by the way we conduct our lives. He says:

> On the surface, it may sound generous, kindhearted, modest, and altruistic. But the view itself is a serious violation of "the way of Jesus," who taught that salvation hinges on hearing and believing His Word (John 5:24). He said, "The words that I speak to you are spirit, and they are life" (John 6:63). To those who doubted his truth claims, He said, "If you do not believe that I am He, you will die in your sins" (John 8:24). He never left any room for someone to imagine that the propositional content of His teaching is optional as long as we mimic His behavior (MacArthur, Truth op.cit. 32-33).

MacArthur continues, "It is not kindness at all, but the worst form of cruelty, to suggest that what people believe doesn't really matter much if they feel spiritual and do good. In fact, on the face of it, that claim is a blatant contradiction of the gospel message" (Ibid. 34).

John MacArthur has a way of putting things in a nutshell. His words:

> Postmodernism is simply the latest expression of worldly unbelief. Its core value ... a dubious ambivalence toward truth ... is merely skepticism distilled to its pure essence. There is nothing virtuous or genuinely humble about it. It is proud rebellion against divine revelation (Ibid. 24).

Not-So-Fast – 10:41 pm: Ouch!

Laurie – 10:42 pm: In the middle of all this is Satan, still attempting to achieve his ultimate goal: to eliminate the gap between himself and God. Ray Yungen, in his book *A Time of Departing*, explains:

> It is important to understand that Satan is not simply trying to draw people to the dark side of a good versus evil conflict. Actually, he is trying to eradicate the gap between himself and God, between good and evil, altogether. When we understand this approach it helps us see why Thomas Merton said everyone is already united with God or why Jack Canfield said he felt God flowing through all things. All means all---nothing left out. Such reasoning implies that God has given His glory to all of creation; since Satan is part of creation, then he too shares in this glory, and thus is "like the Most High" (108).

Campus Joy – 10:46 pm: This comes together to make evident the rebellion of the ages: Satan against God Almighty. The global interfaith movement is preparing a consensus, a common ground, for all religions to unite in a oneness of spirituality. It is believed that, as we ride the waves of postmodernism, the idea is not to search for safe middle ground, but to ride those waves, then bridge opposites, especially where there is hope for convergence in compromise and enlightenment (Sweet, Soul 163).

Roger Oakland responds by saying that bridging the opposites refers to the chasm that separates good and evil. This tension between good and evil is called dualism, and Satan's goal is to eradicate it. If only that gap could be closed, then Satan and God would be equal (Oakland, op. cit. 186).

Notice what the Word of God has to say concerning this:

How are you fallen from heaven, O Lucifer, son of the morning! How you are cut down to the ground, you who weakened the nations! For you have said in your heart: "I will ascend into heaven, I will exalt my throne above the stars of God; I will also sit on the mount of the congregation. On the farthest sides of the north; I will ascend above the heights of the clouds, I will be like the Most High." Yet you shall be brought down to Sheol, to the lowest depths of the Pit (Isaiah 14:12-15).

Looking to nature for metaphors, we can say that seismic events, in response to the postmodern earthquake, have ushered in a tsunami which has brokered a whole new world. The earth is in transition now and in the process of transforming from *terra firma* into *terra incognita*. Since we are navigating in a totally new setting, there are many transformations to be made in order for us to live in this new site and share in religious shifts inherent in the transition. This could be regarded as Postmodern Reformation (Sweet, Soul, op.cit. 17).

Square-Away – 11:07 pm: Well, blow me down, Boys, there's nothing subtle about this idea from Leonard Sweet.

Brother Carviss – 11:09 pm: A surreptitious strategy in progressing into this Postmodern Reformation is to indoctrinate seminary leaders and professors in the postmodern contemplative experience. Then we just watch as thousands of ordained missiologists go about re-imaging Christ followers into clones for the New Spirituality. An informative web search: track the Christian colleges and universities who currently promote this New Contemplative Spirituality by multi-media and experiential enlightenment. Interestingly, a web search will also reveal the sects of faith-based groups being led on secular campuses as well.

Now, our marching orders as Bible-believing and trusting Christians come from Jesus, "You are the light of the world. A city that is set on a hill cannot be hidden. Nor do they light a lamp and put it under a basket, but on a lamp stand, and it gives light to all who are in the house" (Matthew 5:14-15).

Our next session is on the "journey" and "how we should really do church." Some books that you may want to reference are: Doug Pagitt's *A Christianity Worth Believing;* DeYoung and Kluck's *Why We're Not Emergent;* Roger Oakland's *Faith Undone*; John MacArthur's *The Truth War*; and Dan Kimball's *The Emerging Church*.

Until next week, August 23rd at 8:00,

Meryl Carviss (blog host)

@chapter_four

IT'S ALL ABOUT THE JOURNEY

> "Let no one deceive himself. If anyone among you seems to be wise in the age, let him become a fool that he may become wise. For the wisdom of this world is foolishness with God. For it is written, 'He catches the wise in their own craftiness;' and again, 'The Lord knows the thoughts of the wise, that they are futile.' Therefore let no one glory in men. ..."
> (1 Corinthians 3:18-21)

AUGUST 23, 2011 - STUDY FORUM BLOGGERS CHECKED IN:

>Brother Carviss >Laurie >Hannah, "Campus-Joy" >Hector, "Not-So-Fast >Will, "Square-Away"

<u>Brother Carviss</u> — 8:00 pm: Another mind-stretching session of blogging — so let's get going! Much of what we'll discuss this evening has to do with perception: is the primary focus of our spiritual walk about the journey or about the destination? Even heavier: can we even be certain of the options of destination or of the existence of any one option?

I once heard a pastor say that he does not refer to himself anymore as a "Christian" since the term has lost much of its original meaning and is a turn-off to this postmodern generation. He said, as if it were original with him, he'd rather be called a "Christ-follower." Now, I know that "Christ-follower" is one of those overlapping terms with various connotations.

A common chord running throughout spiritual formation (particularly contemplative prayer) is that the silence (induced through meditation by mantra) and being a Christ-follower are usually tied together. However, receiving Christ as Savior, Lord, and Master by being "born again" (John 3:12) is not the pre-requisite to being a Christ-follower. Rather, as Richard Foster teaches, in his *Celebration of Discipline*, anyone can practice spiritual disciplines and become like Christ. In this context, our Savior serves as a model to be followed. Yes, Christ is the perfect One, and He gave His Word and His example to guide us, but it is His Spirit within, as a result of being born again, who transforms and gives us the power to be like Him. The crucial point to grasp is that one can join a community of Christ-followers, participate in disciplines of spiritual formation, and even have a feel-good experience as a result of contemplative prayer, and yet never, through repentance and grace because of faith in Christ, never be truly born again. Can we possibly move closer and closer to God without ever taking that step to be truly saved?

<u>Laurie</u> – 8:15 pm: Doug Pagitt, author of *A Christianity Worth Believing*, puts forth two ways of looking at God: He is either "up and out," or He is "down and in." "Up and out" refers to a perfect and unreachable god, while "down and in" refers to deity being "close, involved, and integrated with humanity" (Pagitt, Christianity op. cit.108, 103).

Pagitt also puts forth the question of being able to trust a god who is "up and out." According to Pagitt, it seems that there could be no actual trust in a perfect god who is always looking for a way to punish us for sins. This god may be forgiving, but not forgetting (Ibid. 110-111).

I'd like to share two passages from the Bible that show God's immense mercy, even in our perception of His "up and out" character:

"For as the heavens are high above the earth, so great is His mercy toward those who fear Him. As far as the east is from the west, so far has He removed our transgressions from us" (Psalm 103:11-12).

"I have blotted out, like a thick cloud, your transgressions, and like a cloud, your sins return to Me, for I have redeemed you" (Isaiah 44:22).

I'd like to show that Father God is both "up and out" and "down and in." Jesus, the very Son of God, bore the cross in order to rip the temple veil from top to bottom ("up and out" to "down and in") in order to make a way for sinful humanity to enter the Holy of Holies, receiving complete forgiveness (Mark 15:38). As a result, we receive the grace to live a trusting, pleasing life because we are clothed in the righteousness of Christ. His grace gives us the power to live a life of belief and trust in God Almighty!

Terms underlying many emerging church conversations, though perhaps seldom named, are "holistic spirituality" and "Pantheistic belief." While each of these terms has its own host of connotations, a common stream of thought would be that God and the material world are one and the same entity. Therefore God is present in everything and all of creation is an integral part of God. This leads to an acceptance and worship of many deities. Thus, we may hear it declared that "the journey" is holistic, as well as Pantheistic.

<u>Square-Away</u> – 8:26 pm: How energizing to me is the belief that Father God is "up and out," "down and in," "above and beneath," "completing surrounding me!" I'm still reading Kevin DeYoung and Ted Kluck's book, *Why We're Not Emergent (By Two Guys Who Should Be)*. I notice how they observed journey and destination. For the emergent, they imply that the destination seems to matter little to postmoderns, since the journey is the most important part. Emerging Christians see the journey of the Christian life as less about our pilgrimage through this fallen world, and more about a wild, uncensored venture of mystery and paradox. Emergents see their role as travelers on an unknown course rather than as "tour guides" who know where they're going and stay the course (DeYoung and Kluck, op. cit. 32).

According to a quote attributed to Dave Tomlinson in *Why We're Not Emergent*:

In much of emergent thought, however, the destination is a secondary matter, as is any concern about being on the right path. Dave Tomlinson states, "Evangelism, therefore, should be seen as an opportunity to 'fund' people's spiritual journeys, drawing on the highly relevant resources of 'little pieces' of truth contained in the Christian narrative" (qtd. in DeYoung and Kluck, op. cit. 33).

Going on, DeYoung explains that in the postmodern world of spiritual journey, authenticity and sincerity have become the currency of authority. Therefore dysfunction, inconsistency, and idiosyncrasy are worn as banners of honor (DeYoung and Kluck, op. cit. 35).

Campus Joy – 8:33 pm: I also have been reading DeYoung and Kluck's book, and I'm drawn to what Kevin DeYoung has to say about the place of "mystery" and "doubt" in the journey:

> Because of the emerging church's implied doctrine of God's unknowability, the word *mystery*, a perfectly good word in its own right, has become downright annoying. Let me be very clear: I don't understand everything about God or the Bible. I don't fully understand how God can be three in one. I don't completely grasp how divine sovereignty works alongside human responsibility. The Christian faith *is* mysterious. But when we talk about Christianity, we don't start with mystery. It's some combination of pious confusion and intellectual laziness to claim that living in mystery is at the heart of Christianity. Yet, time and again, emerging leaders brand Christianity as, above all things, it seems mysterious (Ibid. 37-38).

De Young also cites that closely related to mystery, another emergent view of journey is that doubt is highlighted as the core of faith. Peter Rollins puts it, "In contrast to the modern view that religious doubt is something to reject, fear or merely tolerate, doubt not only can be seen as an inevitable aspect of our humanity but also can be celebrated as a vital part of faith" (qtd. in DeYoung and Kluck, op.cit. 49).

Square-Away – 8:40 pm: Enlightening, isn't it, that Jesus did not applaud Peter's doubt when walking on the water's surface in the Sea of Galilee? Rather, Jesus asked, "O you of little faith, why did you doubt?" (Matt. 14:31). Nor did Jesus affirm Peter when he doubted what Christ told His disciples was soon to take place: the Gethsemane moment. Peter's anchor was aweigh in response to his reception of Jesus prediction of upcoming events. Jesus was loyal to uncovering the truth that doubt was not the friend of Peter's faith, but rather its enemy (Matthew 16: 21-23)! In fact, we are called to search the Word of God for truth, then to stand on it without wavering or doubting. James exhorts us:

> If any of you lacks wisdom, let him ask of God, who gives to all liberally and without reproach, and it will be given to him. But let him ask in faith, with no doubting, for he who doubts is like a wave of the sea driven and tossed by the wind. For let not that man suppose that he will receive anything from the Lord; he is a double-minded man, unstable in all his ways (James 1:5-8).

Brother Carviss – 8:44 pm: Moving along the journey, some have wondered aloud, "Am I in an emergent church; Am I an emergent Christian?" Kevin DeYoung puts it this way:

> You might be an emergent Christian: ... if you love the Bible as a beautiful, inspiring collection of works that lead us into the mystery of God but is not inerrant; if you search for truth but aren't sure it can be found; ... if you disbelieve in any sacred-secular divide; ... if you long for a community that is relational, tribal, and primal like a river or a garden; if you believe doctrine gets in the way of an interactive relationship with Jesus; if you believe who goes to hell is no one's

business and no one may be there anyway; if you believe salvation has a little to do with atoning for guilt and a lot to do with bringing the whole creation back into shalom with its Maker; if you believe following Jesus is not believing the right things but living the right way; if it really bugs you when people talk about going to heaven instead of heaven coming to us; if you disdain monological, didactic preaching; if you use the word 'story' in all your propositions about postmodernism – if all or most of this tortuously long sentence describes you, then you might be an emergent Christian (DeYoung and Kluck, op. cit. 21-22).

Laurie – 8:49 pm: I've been reading a book, *Listening To The Beliefs Of Emerging Churches*, by general editor Robert Webber. The work is a compilation of emergent conversations by some of the leading authors and pastors of today's emergent church. The first passage I'll share is a paraphrase from John Burke's opinion about moral code. While ministering at a pragmatic modern church, John Burke worked to begin "Axis," a church within a church to draw the emerging generation. Burke explains that moral codes for most world religions are similar. He reasons that it's as if this general understanding of right and wrong comes from within all people. Therefore, Burke sees this innate moral code as common ground on which believers of various world religions can agree (Webber 51).

Mark Driscoll, who has pulled away from some of the extremes of the total emergent movement, cautions that, according to Martin Luther, religion and morality are the default mechanisms of the human heart that is trying to be righteous apart from Jesus Christ (Ibid. 70).

Driscoll goes on to say that Christianity is not like other world religions (Ibid. 71-72):

Christianity is Jesus Christ---

- Resurrected

- Reigning and ruling over all times and people
- Distinct from and superior to all others
- Jesus Christ, in fact, speaks for Himself---
- Jesus said He was God (John 8:58-59; 10:30-33; 14:8-9)
- Jesus said He came from heaven (John 6:38; 16:28)
- Jesus said He was sinless (John 8:46)
- Jesus forgave sin (Mark 2:5)
- Jesus said He was the only way to heaven (John 11:25; 14:6)

<u>Brother Carviss</u> – 9:00 pm: As we reflect on the emergent journey, we can see that compromise has led to unbelief and heresy. John MacArthur speaks to how subtle this turning can be. John says that inerrancy is often defined as the freedom from error or untruths, as in infallibility, especially when referring to the Bible as containing no mistakes. Many emerging Christians, however, appear to move away from the opinion of inerrancy of the Bible, seeking rather to just follow the examples of morality as Jesus has demonstrated in that same Bible. The general understanding among many emerging churches is that indeed God has spoken to us through His Word, but that He is still speaking today, just as authoritatively, through other means. For example:

> Grenz and Franke argue that the Spirit of God speaks through Scripture, tradition, and culture, and theologians must seek to hear the voice of the Spirit in each one. Moreover, since culture is constantly in flux, they say, it is right and fitting for Christian theology to be in a perpetual state of transition and ferment too. No issue should ever be regarded as finally settled (MacArthur, Truth, op.cit. 19).

Therein is the deception of the journey: spreading the foundation with truth, next interjecting enough mendacity to cause confusion and doubt, then finishing the top layer with a solution of "light" that is "dark!"

Not-So-Fast – 9:13 pm: I had begun to wonder if I'd get a word in crosswise tonight! Just listening to all of you, along with reading some of these references on my own, I've come to the conclusion that the journey must propose a lot of questions. In fact, it seems that the questions themselves have more importance that any given answer! Anyway, I still kind of like that Ted Kluck and Kevin DeYoung duo. Ted is especially funny, and together they help keep my head from spinning off my shoulders with all this heavyweight discussion! See how many can follow this train:

> ... theology, for many in the emerging church, becomes something different from speaking the truth about God as revealed in Scripture. The task of theology, in the emergent model, is to express communal beliefs and values, to set forth that community's particular "web of significance" and "matrix of meaning." ... Might they also get the Word of God just as authoritatively somewhere else? Does that make the Bible one of many authorities in the community? ... Does doctrine speak of what is objectively true and corresponds to reality, or does it merely set the rules of discourse and explain our belief mosaic (DeYoung and Kluck, op. cit. 79-80)?

Campus-Joy – 9:19 pm: The questions are valid, Hector, but what of the answers? Drawing us back to accountability, Kevin DeYoung further reveals:

> It sounds cool to say that God is present and absent, nowhere and now here, but once the "tension" and "complexity" of these epigrams wear off, you're left wondering, "Uh?" Maybe that's the point. New life will emerge from the "Uh?" But this is so unlike Paul's actual sermon at Mars Hill. After Paul did his cultural engagement thing, he proclaimed the gospel in no uncertain terms. "The times of ignorance God overlooked, but now he commands all people everywhere to repent, because he has fixed a day on which he will judge the world in

righteousness by a man whom he has appointed; and of this he has given assurance to all by raising him from the dead" (Acts 17:30-31) (DeYoung and Kluck, op. cit. 109).

<u>Campus-Joy</u> – 9:25 pm: In all of our searching and blogging, I challenge each of us to keep before us a statement of the apostle Paul, "For the word of God is quick, and powerful, and sharper than any two-edged sword, piercing even to the dividing asunder of soul and spirit, and of the joints and marrow, and is a discerner of the thoughts and intents of the heart" (Hebrews 4:12).

Seeing that the Word of God is this powerful, then we know it is stable and eternal in its scope. God, the all-powerful One is the Author of Scripture, and He is beyond all time, culture, and social formation. Contextualizing teaches that people and cultures must change, and therefore God's Word must change also. Actually, it's the people who must change to conform to God's Word. In the same way, the Word of God is also a living mechanism that is not to be altered---rather it alters the reader's life and heart. Christianity is so much more than just putting words around people's experiences. Any faithful student of the Bible knows that God is always right, and it is humans who are often wrong. Therefore, when we trust human consensus, we'll be left with man's perspective and not God's true revelation. This is both a dangerous and irresponsible way to develop one's spiritual life, since the outcome can lead to blinding deception (Oakland, op. cit. 44-45).

<u>Square-Away</u> – 9:40 pm: The unaltered Word of God is offensive to unbelievers, just as the apostle Paul stated, "For the preaching of the cross is to them that perish foolishness; but unto us which are saved it is the power of God" (1 Corinthians 1:18).

If Paul had been contextualizing or adjusting Scripture to appease the culture and context of the lives of those to whom he spoke, he would not have referred to unbelievers as foolish and perishing. Paul was absolutely sure that God's Word, unchanged, could reach into the soul and heart of any person who would be willing to receive Jesus Christ, by faith. No matter a person's state in life, the Gospel of Christ will provide God's love, forgiveness and eternal life to all who believe.

Contextual theology is cutting edge thought for many emerging churches. The idea is that the Bible is not standing on its own, but other factors such as history, culture, and ethnicity must be recognized, and along with these factors the message of the Bible must be tailored to fit current times. In other words, let the Christian's life mold the Bible rather than having the Bible mold the Christian's life. In determining to accomplish contextual theology, we see communities of emergent believers move away from Bible teaching and move into a dialectic stance. By this, I mean that instead of just one person teaching biblical doctrine, all members may express an opinion and thereby come to a consensus of what the Bible might mean in a given passage (Oakland, op. cit. 42-43).

In Doug Pagitt's *Church Re-Imagined*, the explanation is made that a genuine community of believers will share in serving the portions of God's Word much as friends do when hurrying to the table of a mouth-watering potluck meal. Belief-building goals are met when the community engages, when sharing their hopes, dreams, and understandings, with the story of God (Pagitt, Church 167).

In a nutshell, contextualizing means that people and cultures change; therefore, God's Word must likewise change. In truth, it's people who need to change to conform to God's Word. One could also say that God's Word is a living mechanism that is not to be altered---instead God's Word alters the reader's life and heart (Oakland, op. cit. 44-45).

Campus-Joy – 9:47 pm: Along this journey, we meet up with new terms which are actually very old terms. There is a concept known as "ancient future," which ascribes truth to the mystic rituals of early Celts, Catholics, monks and mystics. Roger Oakland puts it this way, "What is tragic is that the Word of God is being replaced with a sensual spirituality, and that means that millions of lost souls will miss the chance to hear the Word of God but will think they are getting truth because it makes them feel good" (Ibid. 60-61).

Some examples of ancient future worship include prayer stations, labyrinths, and drumming circles. Oakland describes:

> The labyrinth is a maze-like structure that is growing in popularity, used during times of contemplative prayer. The participant walks through this structure until he comes to the center, then back out again. Unlike a maze, which has several paths, the labyrinth has one path. Often *prayer stations* (with candles, icons, pictures, etc.) can be visited along the way. The labyrinth originated in early pagan societies. The usual scenario calls for the pray-er to do some sort of meditation practice, enabling him or her to center down (i.e., reach God's presence), while reaching the center of the labyrinth (Ibid. 67).

<u>Laurie</u> – 9:56 pm: One can see how mysticism is involved in the evolution of the New Spirituality. Mystical practices have been invited into the church through ancient, as well as contemporary, Catholic mystics such as Thomas Merton (1915-1968) and Henri Nouwen (1932-1996). I well remember first hearing about some of the New Age teachings in the 70's and 80's. As we discussed this in Bible study classes, no one suspected that New Age Christianity would ever be attempted and accepted as a "new reformation" in the decades immediately following.

Going on, we see that Drumming Circles are a prime example of the seemingly innocent gathering of people who enjoy the feeling of belonging to a musical group and yet are being led into a mystical state, while moving out of their heads. This shamanistic-type drumming is purposed as a way to enter a mystical state. While releasing one's brain into a hypnotic state, the beat of a drum may "speak directly to the intelligence of the body" (Ibid. 69-70).

Its wide range of functions include the promotion of harmony with your inner self, with other people and with nature, relaxation and healing from stress, the invoking of spirit guides and the promotion of cosmic energy flow, an aid to meditation and the attaining of trances, and also, in more aggressive styles of drumming, the arousing of various wild passions. The latter may even take the form of revolt against society and its norms (qtd. in Oakland, op. cit. 69-71).

<u>Not-So-Fast</u> – 10:03 pm: In reading Dan Kimball's *The Emerging Church*, I related to some of the physical surroundings that are typically created. One will find that a part of the setting for many emerging church services is a darkened auditorium or room. This is accomplished with black paint on walls and ceilings, heavy black curtains covering windows, and a lowering or lack of artificial light during part or all of the gathering time. We learn that darkness symbolizes spirituality in emerging culture, particularly in Buddhist temples, and some Catholic and Orthodox churches (Kimball 136).

I really liked the idea of meditation being worked into the new postmodern worship! In college, I dabbled into some forms of Eastern religions, and was fascinated by them. I've done some extra research, and have found that a much used spiritual discipline of many emerging churches is contemplative prayer (or contemplative spirituality). Contemplative prayer can be defined as a belief system that uses ancient mystical meditation practices to induce altered states of consciousness (also known as the silence). This discipline has grown from a concept called spiritual formation, made popular by Richard Foster in his 1978 best seller, *Celebration of Discipline*. Further, Foster recommends a book by Tilden Edwards, founder of the Shalom Institute in Washington, DC. Edwards explains that contemplative prayer is what bridges Eastern religions with Christianity. Edwards speaks of this mystical bridge: "[T]he more popular Eastern impact in the West through transcendental meditation, Hatha Yoga, the martial arts, and through many available courses on Eastern religions in universities, has aided a recent rediscovery of Christian apophatic mystical tradition" (qtd. in Oakland, op. cit. 86).

Square-Away – 10:10 pm: Hector, those who practice or teach contemplative prayer explain that the purpose is to tune in with God and hear His voice. However, Richard Foster claims that practitioners must use caution. He admits that in contemplative prayer "we are entering deeply into the spiritual realm" and that sometimes it is not the realm of God even though it is "supernatural." He relates there are spiritual beings and that a prayer of protection should be said beforehand, something to the effect of, "All dark and evil spirits must now leave" (Ibid. 99).

It seems to me that Christians and non-Christians alike, are susceptible to communication and influence with any number of spiritual options when entering the "common to man" spiritual realm.

In further reading on this topic, I found that Tony Campolo, a prolific author who often speaks at emerging church events, makes these statements in his book, *Speaking My Mind*:

> Beyond these models of reconciliation, a theology of mysticism provides some hope for common ground between Christianity and Islam. Both religions have within their histories examples of ecstatic union with God…I do not know what to make of the Muslim mystics, especially those who have come to be known as the Sufis. What do they experience in their mystical experiences? Could they have encountered the same God we do in our Christian mysticism (qtd. in Oakland, op. cit. 108)?

Brother Carviss – 10:14 pm: John MacArthur notes the current thrust to make Christianity more contemporary and sophisticated in order to reach this present culture. He sees the effort as disastrous, as the postmodern culture grows increasingly hostile toward authority, clarity, and authoritative proclamations of the truth. Following this, evangelicalism is carelessly drifting more and more into postmodernism, thinking this will enable them to reach the present culture. As a result, the church is progressively less willing to fight for truth (MacArthur, Truth, op. cit. 48).

A nugget on relativism from John MacArthur:
> Postmodernism therefore signals a major triumph for relativism ... the view that truth is not fixed and objective, but something individually determined by each person's unique, subjective perception. All this is ultimately a vain attempt to try to eliminate morality and guilt from human life (Ibid. 13).

I've been thinking: As we journey together, is it a coincidence or diabolical planning that postmodern science and spiritually have locked arms in order to lead us down fractal paths toward global unity from the chaos of the 21st Century?

Laurie – 10:20 pm: We addressed quantum physics to some degree a couple of weeks ago. For some time now, I've been exploring and listening to speakers regarding this "new science." Recently, I viewed a 2004 film, *What The Bleep Do We Know?* It took a few times around before I got much out of it. I've tried to remember, as best I can, some highlights of what I understand about quantum physics:

- Quantum physics is about possibilities, not absolutes;
- Rather than matter being stable and reliable, we now know that particles (smaller than atoms and sometimes faster than the speed of light) can appear and disappear at unexplained times and ways;
- Electrons, as well as the nuclei of atoms are moving in and out of existence, maybe even transferring from one universe to the other;

- Using quantum physics, the most important thing to realize is that we are all one, and we are connected to everything and everyone else. We are all meshed with time, space, and the universes;
- All of us will one day reach the place of avatars (incarnations of Hindu deities), such as the Buddhas or Jesus or Mohammed;
- Quantum physics rests on the premise that nothing is absolute, that what we were sure we knew is now "proven" to be wrong. This is all coordinated perfectly with New Age Spirituality;
- Quantum physics teaches that God is too big, too intelligent, too awesome to ever be offended by mere humans who do wrong. In fact, there is no right or wrong;
- Why would God condemn humans when we are all "Gods?" According to quantum physics and the New Spirituality, God is in all things of creation, so therefore, we are all in God which makes us "Gods;"
- As we humans design what we want in our reality, we must learn to lose ourselves in focus and consciousness until we lose our very identity. Then as choices becomes ours, we realize that we are co-creating our future with God;
- If science can discover areas of "certainty," now changed because of new technological research, then religion can also be revolutionized by this new scientific knowledge: God is in everything, so everything is God.

Not to leave out the children, Brian Greene has written a children's book entitled, *Icarus At The Edge Of Time*. A futuristic reimagining of a classic Greek myth, Greene's book relates the tale of an adventurous boy who flashes through space and challenges the overwhelming power of black holes. In an advertising spot, Greene recommended reading the beautiful book, illustrated with photos from the Hubble Space Telescope, to young children. Then at a later time in childhood, the science of quantum physics can be introduced, using the Icarus legend.

Brother Carviss — 10:38 pm: That's timely, Laurie, because the question has come up regarding the place fractals have in quantum physics. I'm going to include some information on the postulates of Chaos Theory and Fractal Order at this time.

Chaos Theory:

New Age belief insists that much of the chaos in this world results from people not properly perceiving the "interconnectedness" of all things (Smith, Wonderful, op. cit. 143).

We've been subtly introduced to the New Age/New Spirituality as a worldview that emphasizes that "chaos" can be noticeably overcome when humanity stops seeing itself as "separate" but rather sees itself as "One"—as a part of the "God" who is "in" everyone and everything (Ibid., 144).

Interestingly, the Bible teaches that humanity is not "God" or "One" with God (John 2:24-25; Ezekiel 28:2; Hosea 11:9).

Fractal Order:

"At any given moment, life is completely senseless. But viewed over a period, it seems to reveal itself as an organism existing in time, having a purpose, trending in a certain direction" (Smith, Wonderful, op. cit. 142).

New discoveries in the science and mathematics of Chaos research are revolutionizing our world view. They reveal a hidden fractal order underlying all seemingly chaotic events. The fractals are intricate and beautiful. They repeat basic patterns, but with an infinity of variations and forms. The world view emerging from this scientific research is new, and yet at the same time ancient (Ibid. 143).

Upon researching this, one could see the deceptive New Age ploy regarding the word fractal and its relationship to 'as above, so below.'...

The word fractal is being used as a pseudo-scientific synonym for the belief that God is 'in' everything—everything being a fractal or a fractured part of the whole, a fractured part of God" (Ibid. 144).

Finally, from MacArthur's book, *The Truth War*:

> ...What we desperately need today are "shepherds according to [God's] heart, who will feed [believers] with knowledge and understanding" (Jeremiah 3:15; Acts 20:28-31). But it is every believer's solemn duty to resist every attack on the truth, to abhor the very thought of falsehood, and not to compromise in any way with the enemy, who is above all a liar and father of lies (John 8:44) (xviii).

We'll call it a night with that timely call from John MacArthur. Next week we'll look at "The Gentle Lion: Heaven and Hell." Books we'll use as reference include Brian McLaren's *The Secret Message of Jesus*, DeYoung and Kluck's *Why We're Not Emergent*, Rob Bell's *Velvet Elvis and Sex God*, and Webber's compilation entitled *Listening to the Beliefs of Emerging Churches*.

Until we meet on Tuesday, August 30th at 8:00 pm,

Meryl Carviss (blog host)

@chapter_five

THE GENTLE LION: HEAVEN AND HELL

> "My sheep hear My voice, and I know them, and they follow Me. And I give them eternal life, and they shall never perish; neither shall anyone snatch them out of My hand." (John 10:27-28)

AUGUST 30, 2011 - STUDY FORUM BLOGGERS CHECKED IN:

>Brother Carviss >Laurie >Hannah, "Campus-Joy" >Hector, "Not-So-Fast" >Will, "Square-Away"

<u>Brother Carviss</u> — 8:00 pm: Have you ever thought of how a stately, strategic, ruling lion could also be a gentle, submissive, vulnerable lamb? This is exactly the unique double role of our Lord and Savior, Jesus Christ! Kevin DeYoung leads us into a paradoxical description of a gentle lion:

> Aslan the lion, the Christ figure in the Chronicles of Narnia, is grandly multidimensional. He's loving, but he's not safe. He's good and terrible at the same time. Susan and Lucy want to bury their heads in his mane and feel his breath. But they also go "trembly" at the sight of him. In one place, Lewis describes Aslan's paw touching the Pevensie children, saying, "And though it was velveted, it was very heavy" (DeYoung and Kluck, op. cit. 248).

In the Bible, Jesus is referred to as both the Lamb of God and the Lion of Judah (John 1:29, Revelation 5:5).

Thinking again of C.S. Lewis' Chronicles of Narnia, I'm reminded of Aslan's appearance. The Lion's courtly majesty is said to be evident in his persona. All beings instinctively offer deference to him. The faithful bow to his lordship. The evil must cower in his presence. Aslan is huge: the size, we are told, of a small elephant. On occasion in the stories, Aslan physically grows in their presence. His being offers light as well as authority. Aslan's velvet paws can be cuddly in their compassion or horrible in their clawed wrath. Aslan is the generous Protector of all that is good and the final and fair Judge of those who refuse grace (Scriptorium Novum On-Line).

Not-So-Fast – 8:12 pm: Hey that Narnia stuff is cool! My two nieces have dragged me to every one of those movies! That Aslan character has always been a mystery to me. I'll have to confess that he is rather alluring.

Brother Carviss – 8:17 pm: Jesus' first coming was as a lamb, who by the blood of His death, took away the sins of the world. His second coming will show Jesus as a lion, the Lion of Judah, who is worthy to receive all power and riches and wisdom, and strength and honor and glory and blessing (Revelation 5:12). In Revelation, we can see a preview of our Lord Jesus Christ as King of Kings and Lord of Lords, ready to call mankind into accountability:

> Then I saw heaven opened, and behold, a white horse. And He who sat on him was called Faithful and True, and in righteousness He judges and makes war. His eyes were like a flame of fire, and on His head were many crowns. He had a name written that no one knew except Himself. He was clothed with a robe dipped in blood, and His name is called The Word of God. And the armies in heaven, clothed in fine linen, white and clean, followed Him on white horses. Now out of His mouth goes a sharp sword, that with it He should

strike the nations. And He Himself will rule them with a rod of iron. He Himself treads the winepress of the fierceness and wrath of Almighty God. And He has on His robe and on His thigh a name written: KING OF KINGS AND LORD OF LORDS (Revelation 19:11-16).

<u>Laurie</u> – 8:25 pm: Yes, Jesus is the gentle one, whose life was given to save us, but He is also the lion who will participate in the judgment of those who deny His grace.

I recently heard a pastor describe sin as not what we do wrong, but rather, sin is missing God's best for our lives. Rob Bell describes hell this way:

> Now if there is a life of heaven, and we can choose it, then there's also another way. A way of living out of sync with how God created us to live. The word for this is hell: a way, a place, a realm absent of how God desires things to be. We can bring heaven to earth; we can bring hell to earth (Bell, Velvet, op. cit.147).

Bell goes on to explain that famine, debt, loneliness, oppression, death, slaughter, and despair are all examples of hell on earth. He further admonishes Christians to resist hell on earth by combating such conditions as poverty, suffering, and injustice in opposing them with all our energies (Bell, Velvet, op. cit. 148).

Understanding the truth of Scripture about the Lion of heaven and hell is tantamount to living this life on earth in the best possible way!

In 1 Peter 2:21-24, the apostle described the cross as the model for our suffering and the payment for our sin. Many see the cross as very simply the place where Jesus absorbed our pain and heartache. The Bible, however, clearly states that Jesus was actually made to be sin for us. "Therefore we are ambassadors for Christ, as though God were pleading through us; we implore you on Christ's behalf, be reconciled to God. For He made Him who knew no sin to be sin for us, that we might become the righteousness of God in Him" (2 Corinthians 5:20-21).

<u>Square-Away</u> – 8:40 pm: To me, 2 Corinthians 5:20-21 is one of the clearest and most powerful verses in the Bible. It is so hard to take in the truth of the trade-off between Jesus Christ and us, and yet we know with our whole being that it is accomplished and we are most blessed!

<u>Brother Carviss</u> – 9:10 pm: The apostle Paul demonstrated the urgency of faithfulness when he emphasized:

> I marvel that you are turning away so soon from Him who called you in the grace of Christ, to a different gospel, which is not another; but there are some who trouble you and want to pervert the gospel of Christ. But even if we, or an angel from heaven, preach any other gospel to you than what we have preached to you, let him be accursed (Galatians 1:6-8).

As in the first century, A.D., we also are faced with discerning various gospels today. We each are called to explain the hope that is ours in regard to salvation. Some explanations of that hope are:

Words From The Bible:

Jesus death accomplished many goals, some of which are found in these passages of the Holy Bible:

- Ephesians 5:2, 25; Galatians 2:20 (<u>to show His love for us</u>)
- Ephesians 2:14-16 (<u>to destroy hostility between races</u>)
- Titus 2:14 (<u>to create a people passionate for good works</u>)
- Hebrews 9:28 (<u>to rescue us from final judgment</u>)
- Romans 3:24, 28; 5:9 (<u>to provide the basis for our justification</u>)

- Philippians 2:8; 3:9; Romans 5:19; 2 Corinthians 5:21 (<u>to complete the obedience that becomes our righteousness</u>).

Rob Bell's Thoughts:

> The fact that we are loved and accepted and forgiven in spite of everything we have done is simply too good to be true. Our choice becomes this: We can trust his retelling of the story, or we can trust our telling of our story. It is a choice we make every day about the reality we are going to live in.
>
> And this reality extends beyond this life.
>
> Heaven is full of forgiven people.
>
> Hell is full of forgiven people.
>
> Heaven if full of people God loves, whom Jesus died for.
>
> Hell is full of forgiven people God loves, whom Jesus died for.
>
> The difference is how we choose to live, which story we choose to live in, which version of reality we trust. Ours or God's (Bell, Velvet, op. cit. 146).

Further, Bell teaches that, as we choose God's vision of our reality, we are flowing into how we'll live for eternity. Therefore, this becomes the life of heaven here and now. By our choices, we can bring heaven to earth or we can bring hell to earth. Bell defines hell as a place, a way or realm absent of how God wants things to be. Hell could be demonstrated by slaughter, death, despair, oppression, loneliness, debt, famine, poverty, or injustice. Bell insists that Jesus wants us to use all our energies to oppose these examples of hell on earth (Ibid. 147-148).

Bell continues by explaining that Jesus measures our eternal standings in terms of not what we say or believe, but how we live, especially in regard to this hell around us. The people who give food to the hungry and water to those that thirst will be the kind of people who spend eternity with God. Conversely, those who don't take care of the needy and hurting in their midst are choosing hell, and God gives them what they want. It follows that by not being generous enough with the poor, we bring hell to earth (Ibid. 148-149).

More specifically, "A Christian is someone who anticipates spending forever here, in a new heaven that comes to earth. The goal isn't escaping this world but making this world the kind of place God can come to. And God is remaking us into the kind of people who can do this kind of work" (Ibid. 150).

Brian McLaren's Thoughts:

Brian McLaren speaks of "our evolution to godliness." In his *Secret Message of Jesus,* McLaren explains the "getting it, getting in" strategies toward becoming a Christ-follower.

- Hear from the heart, thinking and rethinking all that you have known as it compares to the secret message. Be willing to change your former thinking. This step is called repentance.
- Move in faith, believing and trusting in God.
- Stay open to receive God's spirit.
- Go public with your repentance, faith, and receptivity.
- Practice following Jesus every day of your life (105-112).

Doug Pagitt's Thoughts:

> ...sin is not the point. We do not live life to manage sin. We live life to join with God, and when sin comes knocking at the door or crouches in the corner or rises from within us, we seek to do away with it. We flee from it. We eradicate it. We plot against it. Sin is not what makes us human. Sin destroys

our humanity and all the rest of creation (Pagitt, *Christianity*, op. cit. 164).

Regardless of how it comes – whether through our habits and systems, our intentions or the doing of others, or our bodies and biology – we live with sin. But we also live with the possibility of freedom from sin. The good news in all this is that sin never gets the last word. We can live our lives in a collective way, so the systems that cause disharmony with God can be changed. We can change the patterns wired into us from our families and create new ways of relating and being. Our bodies can experience healing. In other words, we can be born-again, new creations (Ibid. 166-167).

Paul the Apostle's Thoughts:

But God demonstrates His own love toward us, in that while we were still sinners, Christ died for us. Much more then, having now been justified by His blood, we shall be saved from wrath through Him. For if when we were enemies we were reconciled to God through the death of His Son, much more, having been reconciled we shall be saved by His life. And not only that, but we also rejoice in God through our Lord Jesus Christ, through whom we have now received the reconciliation (Romans 5:8-11).

Square-Away – 9:30 pm: John MacArthur, author of *The Truth War*, asserts that in our present culture of ambiguity, people often resist authoritative biblical truth, especially as the truth works to correct worldly lifestyles and ungodly behavior.

Not knowing what you believe (especially on a matter as essential to Christianity as the gospel) is by definition a kind of unbelief. Refusing to acknowledge and defend the revealed truth of God is a particularly stubborn and pernicious kind of unbelief. Advocating ambiguity, exalting uncertainty, or otherwise deliberately clouding the truth is a sinful way of nurturing unbelief (MacArthur, Truth, op. cit. xi)

Bottom Line: God is holy. We are not. His gentle, velvety lion paws made a way of redemption for us because of His love for us, His creation. If we refuse this matchless grace, our holy God does have claws with which he continuously draws us back to Him in love. If, however, we continually refuse His grace, there will come a time of eternal separation from that Gentle Lion.

Not-So-Fast – 9:56 pm: There's that "separation" word again. That's the word that means we're not getting the idea of the "new way." I think more of this is coming up. I rather enjoy being a loner, so we'll see if I can swallow this "separation" stuff!

Brother Carviss – 10:10 pm: DeYoung reminds us:

> We need to know Jesus Christ as both Lion and Lamb. The lionlike Jesus in Matthew 23 who said, "Woe to you, teachers of the law and Pharisees, you hypocrites! You travel over land and sea to win a single convert, and when he becomes one, you make him twice as much a son of hell as you are," is the same Christ as the lamblike Jesus in Matthew 25 who said, "I tell you the truth, whatever you did for one of the least of these brothers of mine, you did for me." And the lamblike Jesus in Matthew 27 who cried out, "My God, my God, why have you forsaken me?" is the same Lord as the lionlike Jesus in Matthew 28 who declared, "All authority in heaven and on earth has been given to me." We need to worship lionlike, lamblike Jesus and glory in all His attributes (DeYoung and Kluck, op. cit. 251-252).

Laurie – 10:15 pm: I've been reading a book by Warren Smith, *False Christ Coming – Does Anybody Care?* I've captured many quotations from this book, most of which are quotes by New Age/New Spirituality authors who give their predictions of "things to come." Remarkably, the vocabulary terms are many times identical to words used in the Holy Bible, but the meanings are vastly different. I've asked Hannah (Campus-Joy) to work with me on this. I'll give the information from *False Christ Coming – Does Anybody Care?* Hannah will match the terms with biblical witness, showing us how the Holy Bible uses the same terms. We'll call this our "Sleight-Of-Hand" vocabulary.

Laurie – 10:18 pm: I'll begin with the term, "Transformation."

Recorded from Hubbard's "Christ" in *The Revelation*: "You must demonstrate the psychological state of universal consciousness as a new norm. That is the first purpose of writing…The second purpose of these writings is to call for the completion of the good news concerning the transformation of the world" (Hubbard 74).

Campus-Joy – 10:22 pm: "Transformation"

"And do not be conformed to this world, but be transformed by the renewing of your mind, that you may prove what is that good and acceptable and perfect will of God" (Romans 12:2).

Laurie – 10:25 pm: "Yours is the power, Yours is the glory"

Recorded from Hubbard's "Christ" in *The Revelation*: "I did not suffer on the cross and rise again on the third day to show you what I could do, but what you can do. Yours is the power, Yours is the glory. That is my message to you" (Hubbard, op. cit. 100)! "You were born to be me, You were born to be partners with God" (Ibid. 148). "The church is the body of believers who are conscious of being me" (Ibid. 102).

Campus-Joy – 10:29 pm: "Yours is the power, Yours is the glory"

Jesus Christ taught His disciples to pray like this:

Our Father in heaven, hallowed be Your name. Your kingdom come. Your will be done on earth as it is in heaven. Give us this day our daily bread. And forgive us our debts, as we forgive our debtors. And do not lead us into temptation, but deliver us from the evil one. For Yours is the kingdom and the power and the glory forever. Amen (Matthew 6: 9-13).

<u>Laurie</u> – 10:35 pm: "Master"

Recorded from Hubbard's "Christ" in *The Revelation*:

It is not that you must wait for some master from without. You all have the same master from within. That master is me, your higher self, the Christ within each of you who is, right now, hearing the same voice, seeing the same vision of the future, despite all differences of language and culture (Hubbard, op. cit. 243).

<u>Campus-Joy</u> – 10:39 pm: "Master"

The words of Jesus Christ: "Remember the word that I said to you, 'A servant is not greater than his master.' If they persecuted Me, they will also persecute you. If they kept My word, they will keep yours also" (John 15:20).

<u>Laurie</u> – 10:44 pm: "Missing the Mark"

Recorded from Hubbard's "Christ" in *The Revelation*:

The end is near. The old play is almost over. Suffice it to say, that if you do not choose to evolve into a wholesome, co-creative human, then you shall not. ...The only punishment is your self-exclusion from the joy of new life. The only pity is that you are missing the mark and choosing to die unfulfilled (Hubbard, op. cit. 195).

Campus-Joy – 10:48 pm: "Missing the Mark"

"For all have sinned and fall short of the glory of God" (Romans 3:23).

"For the wages of sin is death, but the gift of God is eternal life in Christ Jesus our Lord" (Romans 6:23).

Laurie – 10:52 pm: "Fear"

From Donald Walsch's *Conversations with God: an uncommon dialogue, Book 2*:
> But this paradigm shift will take great wisdom, great courage, and massive determination. For Fear will strike at the heart of these concepts and call them false. Fear will eat at the core of these magnificent truths and make them appear hollow. Fear will distort, disdain, destroy. And so Fear will be your greatest enemy (242).

Campus-Joy – 10:57 pm: "Fear - meaning to listen to God"

"Be not wise in your own eyes; fear the Lord, and depart from evil" (Proverbs 3:7).

"By mercy and truth atonement is provided for iniquity; and by the fear of the Lord one departs from evil" (Proverbs 16:6).

"Fear - meaning the opposite of trusting God"

"Fear not, for I am with you; be not dismayed, for I am your God. I will strengthen you, yes I will help you. I will uphold you with My righteous right hand" (Isaiah 41:10).

Laurie – 11:02 pm: "Satan's Eternal Goal"

Recorded from Hubbard's "Christ" in *The Revelation*: "Tell them to recognize the God within themselves, and to follow that light through the darkness of the tribulations to the dawn of the Universal Age, when only the God-conscious continue to exist, and everyone is like Christ" (Hubbard, op. cit. 102).

<u>Campus-Joy</u> – 11:05 pm: "Satan's Eternal Goal"

> The word of the Lord came to me again, saying, "Son of man, say to the prince of Tyre, 'Thus says the Lord God: Because your heart is lifted up, and you say, I am a god, I sit in the seat of gods, in the midst of the seas, yet you are a man, and not a god, though you set your heart as the heart of a god ...'" (Ezekiel 28:2).

<u>Laurie</u> – 11:09 pm: "Being Separate"

Quoted in Warren Smith's *False Christ Coming - Does Anybody Care?*
"Christ" states that those who see themselves as "separate" and not "divine" hinder humanity's ability to spiritually evolve. Those who deny their own "divinity" are like "cancer cells" in the body of God. "Christ" warns that a healthy body must have no cancer cells. Cancer cells must be healed or completely removed from the body. He describes the means of removal as the "selection process." The "selection process" results in the deaths of those who refuse to see themselves as a part of God" (qtd. in Smith , False 28).

<u>Campus-Joy</u> – 11:14 pm: "Being Separate"

> "Come out from among them and be separate," says the Lord. "Do not touch what is unclean, and I will receive you. I will be a Father to you, and you shall be My sons and daughters," says the Lord Almighty (2 Corinthians 6:17).

Brother Carviss — 11:18 pm: Thank you, Laurie and Hannah for your research and for sharing with us. Some are probably thinking about now, "Why dwell so much on New Age terminology? Why don't we just ignore all this New Age stuff, knowing it means nothing." My short answer is that New Age teachers and authors are not just putting unrealistic jargon out there. There is the Holy Spirit and also evil spirits available to man, and in these last days, we must be especially discerning regarding our "companions." Many postmodern church propositions sound a little whacky until one matches them with foundations of New Age/New Spirituality. Warren Smith, the author of *False Christ Coming. Does Anybody Care?* was saved out of New Age. As new Christians in the 1980's, Warren and his wife were shocked to find New Age teachings infiltrating the church. Their ministry, as well as many others today, are committed to raising awareness regarding this New Spirituality, and the dangers of this most virulent of deceptions.

Next week, we'll look at "The New Global Kingdom Of God." We'll also tackle the sin issue which seems kind of "old hat," until we seriously consider the postmodern notion that there is no sin, no right or wrong choices, no way to wander off the correct path since there is neither a correct nor incorrect path. Sources we'll use next session are: McLaren's *A New Kind of Christianity* and *The Secret Message of Jesus*; Rob Bell's *Velvet Elvis*; Pagitt's *A Christianity Worth Believing*; DeYoung and Kluck's *Why We're Not Emergent*.

Until next Tuesday, September 6th at 8:00 pm,

Meryl Carviss (blog host)

@chapter_six

THE NEW GLOBAL KINGDOM OF GOD

"If we say that we have no sin, we deceive ourselves, and the truth is not in us." (1 John 1:8)

September 6, 2011 - STUDY FORUM BLOGGERS CHECKED IN:

>Brother Carviss >Laurie >Hannah, "Campus-Joy" >Hector, "Not-So-Fast" >Will, "Square-Away"

<u>Brother Carviss</u> – 8:00 pm: The topic at hand is the Kingdom of God. I like to say that where Jesus is king, there is the Kingdom of God. As Jesus remains king in my heart, I'm assured that the Kingdom of God is within me!

I'll begin with two scriptures which immediately come to my mind:

"...for the kingdom of God is not food and drink, but righteousness and peace and joy in the Holy Spirit" (Romans 14:17).

"Now when He was asked by the Pharisees when the kingdom of God would come, He answered them and said, 'The kingdom of God does not come with observation;' nor will they say, 'See here!' or 'See there!' For indeed, the kingdom of God is within you" (Luke 17:20-21).

In Brian McLaren's discourse on the Kingdom of God, he is essentially declaring that he experienced a shift from the gospel according to Paul to the gospel according to Jesus: Paul's thesis, shown in his letter to the Romans, that the gospel was the message of justification by grace through faith; Jesus' answer that He came to announce a new kingdom, a new way of life, a new peace ... good news to all people of every religion. In fact, Jesus' new kingdom was much bigger than a religion and even had room for many religious traditions within it...It was a summons to rethink all things and progress through a life of retraining as disciples of this new kingdom (McLaren, New Kind, op. cit. 137, 139).

My question: Where is all of this headed?

<u>Square-Away</u> – 8:10 pm: Well, hang out the battle lantern, we're headed into an interfaith global church (Kingdom of God)! Here's the rhetoric: All religions can enter this kingdom and be united in Christ, as the one who, by His resurrection, got all of creation in sync with the ultimate plan of God. By this, every human is now justified and born again into the life of the ages. Again, all people may keep their own religious traditions, but buy into the totality of the global Kingdom of God. Next, there is a "going public," using any preferred form of baptism. There is the eating of the new Passover (the Eucharist) to continually receive the impartation of Jesus' forgiveness in order to experience liberation from the principalities and powers in heavenly places. Finally, there is the "receiving" of the Kingdom of God by becoming a citizen of this new peaceable kingdom. Citizens act as disciples to learn its ways. They act as apostles to make its presence available to all (Ibid. 140).

McLaren continues:

> After all, we're not importing any strange language into our theology; we're strictly working with what's always been there. We're not claiming some new revelation or new authority figure. We're following the best Christian tradition of going back to Jesus and the Scriptures, so our quest for a new kind of Christianity is, in fact, a most conservative quest. In our return to our roots, however, we're not writing off all the great sages, scholars, and saints of church history. We're simply going back to the original evangelists, apostles, and

especially Jesus and making sure we're as in sync with them as possible from this point forward ... (Ibid. 141).

In checking out synonyms for sages, I noted these nouns: authority, elder, guru, hakam, maharishi, mahatma, master, Nestor, oracle. As the next quote is read the wise will realize we are nearly at "'zero dark thirty," and it's time to trim our lamps!

> ...we're discovering that the more we let Jesus's message of the kingdom of God sink in, the more it begins to unsettle all our existing understandings and categories. It changes everything...At some point, though, more and more of us will finally decide that it would make more sense to go back and revise the contract from scratch. And that process has begun. It is nowhere near complete, but the cat is out of the bag; imaginations are sizzling, and exciting theological work is being done---by theologians, yes, but equally important, by pastors, preachers, songwriters, producers, poets, dramatists, sculptors, photographers, painters, architects, youth leaders, community organizers, moms and dads, and thoughtful readers like you (Ibid. 142).

Bedrock theological transformation is underway, and being accomplished by the list given above?? "Someone get me a drink of Dad's Old Fashioned ---- fast!"

Campus-Joy – 8:25 pm: When confronted with the scripture from John 14:6, "I am the way, and the truth, and the life. No one comes to the father except through me," many postmodern leaders will look to Rob Bell for a response:

> Jesus was not making claims about one religion being better than all other religions. That completely misses the point, the depth, and the truth. Rather, he was telling those who were following him that his way is the way to the depth of reality. This kind of life Jesus was living, perfectly and completely in

connection and cooperation with God, is the best possible way for a person to live. It is how things are....Perhaps a better question than who's right, is who's living rightly (Bell,Velvet, op. cit. 21)?

A word from Doug Pagitt:

> In the judicial model, God must judge us according to the law. But God is allowed to show us mercy as long as the punishment for our wrongdoing is carried out. So God, who is evidently powerless to do otherwise, must offer Jesus as a blood sacrifice in our place. Yes, it breaks God's heart to do it, but what choice does God have? The law is the law (Pagitt, Christianity, op. cit. 154).

Moving on in the New Kingdom of God, Brian McLaren, in *The Secret Message of Jesus*, spoke in several metaphors to describe the Kingdom of God. DeYoung masterfully wove the comparative language in this way:

> For those in the emerging church, Jesus' message of the kingdom is a manifesto about God's plan for humanity here and now. It is the secret and subversive announcement that God is working out His plan for peace, justice and compassion on the earth. The kingdom message is a summons to participate with God in His dream for humanity, His revolution of love and reconciliation. It is an invitation to join the party of God and be a part of His worldwide mission to heal and be healed. It is a call to join the network of God that breaks down the walls of racism, nationalism, and ecological harm. The kingdom of God is like a dance of love, vitality, harmony, and celebration (DeYoung and Kluck, op. cit. 183-184).

A little later, Kevin DeYoung declares:

The emergent emphasis of justice and compassion would be more of a helpful corrective if it went hand in hand with a firm, unashamed belief, made central and upfront, in the reality of everlasting punishment and everlasting reward, the resurrection of all men either to life or judgment, the necessity of faith in Jesus Christ (DeYoung and Kluck, op. cit. 187).

This is probably a good time to introduce Rick Warren's purpose driven plan to bring about world peace and solve humanity's problems. Warren believes that the Kingdom of God is for here and now, and that we are responsible for bringing about that kingdom on earth. Warren's plan is as follows:

> P romoting reconciliation (changed in 2007 from planting churches)
>
> E quip leaders
>
> A ssist the poor
>
> C are for the sick
>
> E ducate the next generation

Not surprising, is the apparent dovetailing of Pastor Warren's Peace Plan with the United Nations' Millennium Development Goals, the latter of which is to be accomplished in accordance with "Keep the Promise–2015" ("Rick Warren's P.E.A.C.E. Plan & the UN Millennium Goals," *crossroad.com*).

Laurie – 8:40 pm: Doug Pagitt has more to say on the topic of the kingdom. Pagitt shares that afterlife-dominant Christianity points out Jesus was once thought to have died and been resurrected so that he could save us from our sins and help us get into God's kingdom someday. In this concept, Jesus was about giving us the key to salvation, which would take place when we entered heaven after death on earth (Pagitt, Christianity, op. cit. 200).

An eye-opening quote from Jesus, himself, "I *am* He who lives, and was dead, and behold, I am alive forevermore. Amen. And I have the keys of Hades and of Death" (Revelation 1:18).

Pagitt continues:

> The way I see it, Jesus was proclaiming something other than a faith of another time and another place. He was not suggesting a competition between here and there, between now and then. No, Jesus was proclaiming a holistic reorganization of all that is and all that will be. He was bringing about a new kind of life that was meant to be lived out right away, right here, and forevermore (Pagitt, Christianity, op. cit. 200).

<u>Square-Away</u> – 8:45 pm: Still going with Doug Pagitt:

> Jesus made it clear that the afterlife isn't a place. It's a state of being. It's the state in which all of God's hopes for the earth, all of God's desires for this partnership with humanity, come to fruition. The kingdom of God is made real in Jesus, the Messiah and Savior. The kingdom isn't somewhere else, waiting for us to die before we can be part of it. It is in us, through us, and for us right here, right now (Ibid. 222).

Old Square-Away's heart is beating with Jesus words of comfort to His disciples:

> Let not your heart be troubled; you believe in God, believe also in Me. In my Father's house are many mansions; if it were not so, I would have told you. I go to prepare a place for you. And if I go and prepare a place for you, I will come again and receive you to Myself; that where I am, there you may be also (John 14:1-3).

Pagitt reiterates that the story of heaven and salvation is based in the reality of this present world, which is the world that God is renewing day by day, and will keep on renewing for all eternity (Pagitt, Christianity, op. cit. 222).

Brother Carviss – 8:55: Packaged closely with this new world view is the definition, or lack thereof, of sin. Sin is a definite issue we must confront, understand, and not miss its purpose and implications.

According to Doug Pagitt, sin is disintegration, or disconnect, with God (who is always near and apparent to us in the world). "If we believe that God is reachable only when we are fully changed, we're stuck with an afterlife-focused faith" (Ibid. 113). Other emergents say sin is not doing what's wrong. It is just our missing what is God's best for our lives.

Square-Away – 9:00 pm: Sin *does* separate us from God: "Behold, the Lord's hand is not shortened, that it cannot save; nor His ear heavy, that it cannot hear. But your iniquities have separated you from your God; and your sins have hidden His face from you, so that He will not hear" (Isaiah 59:2). It is in believing, repenting, and accepting Jesus' sacrifice as the payment for our sin that we are fully changed and then live with the dunamis of Christ in us to do the will of God. This is how the apostle Peter answered those who asked how they could be forgiven and saved:

> Therefore let all the house of Israel know assuredly that God has made this Jesus, whom you crucified, both Lord and Christ. Now, when they heard this, they were cut to the heart, and said to Peter and the rest of the apostles, "Men and brethren, what shall we do?" Then Peter said to them, "Repent, and let every one of you be baptized in the name of Jesus Christ for the remission of sins; and you shall receive the gift of the Holy Spirit" (Acts 2:36-38).

Not-So-Fast – 9:05: This is where I definitely have something to say! In my investigative study of history, I've come to realize that so many concepts we toss around as depravity and sin, as well as salvation are simply traced to 5th Century St. Augustine. He established Christianity as the state religion. He then had to generate the idea of sin (humans with inherent depravity), and the people's ability to escape eternal punishment only by the blood of our risen Christ. Thus Jesus Christ became man's bridge to Holy God (Pagitt, Christianity, op. cit. 126). I agree with Doug Pagitt, who does not acknowledge Jesus as the only way to forgiveness of sin. Rather, Pagitt sees sin as disintegration which is in a continual state of healing. Therefore:

- We seek to do away with sin;
- We flee from sin;
- We eradicate sin;
- We plot against sin (Ibid. 164).

Pagitt further declares that sin in not something which offends God's sensibilities... We don't need punishment, but Karem (healing redemption) (Ibid. 160).

Square-Away – 9:10: Hector, the stance you've chosen on sin is popular among agnostics and atheists. Please take note that Pagitt's plan to obtain healing for the disintegration begins each line with "We…" This is a humanistic view of salvation. I can only answer with the Word of God from His Holy Bible. What is sin?

> Whoever commits sin also commits lawlessness, and sin is lawlessness. And you know that He [God in Jesus] was manifested to take away our sins, and in Him there is no sin. Whoever abides in Him does not sin. Whoever sins has neither seen Him nor known Him. Little children, let no one deceive you. He who practices righteousness is righteous, just as He is righteous. (1 John 3:4-8).

Another passage, 1 John 4:1-6, shows that the Spirit of Antichrist is defined by someone accepting credit for qualities of the fruit of the Spirit, when these attributes are genuinely only from Jesus Christ.

Hector, I ask you to follow me in a few more of Doug Pagitt's quotes, followed by my response, citing the Word of God. Only you can decide who you will believe and to whom you will give your allegiance.

From Pagitt's writing:

> And so it goes with faith. The legal model drives us into places of despair and self-loathing. It creates distance between us and God. It makes us afraid of God and suspicious of others. But when we think of sin as disintegration, as the unraveling of life and goodness, we hold on to the hope that there is healing and integration, that a life can be woven back together from the threads that remain (Pagitt, Christianity, op. cit. 169).

Square-Away - In Christ, we are a new creation, because old things have passed away and all things have become new (2 Corinthians 5:17).

From Pagitt's writing:

"Sin mattered because it was less than what God wanted for humanity" (Pagitt, Christianity, op. cit. 158).

Square-Away - Sin matters because it causes separation from God! Jesus actually "became sin for us." This incomparable trade-off is explained by the apostle Paul, "For He made Him who knew no sin to be sin for us, that we might become the righteousness of God in Him" (2 Corinthians 5:21).

Mark Driscoll says that on the cross, substituting for us, Jesus - the sinless one — "exchanged His perfection for our imperfection, His obedience for our disobedience, His blessing for our cursing, and His life for our death" (Driscoll and Breshears 114).

From Pagitt's writing:

> The doctrine of inherent depravity was, in part, Augustine's effort to explain the necessity of participating in the state

religion – since the church was now official, people could join as a part of their citizenship. Those most committed to the faith felt compelled to help others see that the church was important in its own right, that involvement could be more than just a civic obligation. So the explanation went something like this:

> All people have a need only the church can fill.
> People are born with a problem-depravity.
> That problem can only be rectified by God.

But the only thing was people couldn't get to God because they were inherently evil. So they needed a go-between. The only solution was Jesus, who fixed the problem of the original sin inheritance. And Jesus could only be accessed through the church, which administered the sacrament of baptism. It was baptism as a mean of grace that freed the individual from the ramifications of depravity (Pagitt, Christianity, op. cit. 126-127).

<u>Square-Away</u> – On the other hand, listen to Paul's admonition to young minister, Timothy:

> I charge you therefore before God and the Lord Jesus Christ, who will judge the living and the dead at His appearing and His kingdom: Preach the word! Be ready in season, and out of season. Convince, rebuke, exhort, with all longsuffering and teaching. For the time will come when they will not endure sound doctrine, but according to their own desires, because they have itching ears, they will heap up for themselves teachers; and they will turn their ears away from the truth, and be turned aside to fables (2 Timothy 4:1-4).

From the Old Testament prophet, Isaiah:

> Surely He [Jesus Christ, the Messiah] has borne our griefs and carried our sorrows; yet we esteemed Him stricken, smitten by God, and afflicted. But He was wounded for our transgressions, He was bruised for our iniquities; the chastisement for our peace was upon Him, and by His stripes we are healed. All we like sheep have gone astray; we have turned, every one, to his own way; and the Lord has laid on Him the iniquity of us all (Isaiah 53:4-6).

<u>Brother Carviss</u> — 9:45 pm: To further understand sin, let's look at the author of sin: Satan, sometimes called Lucifer, Angel of Light, and Devil among other names.

Isaiah 14:12-15:

> How you are fallen from heaven, O Lucifer, son of the morning! How you are cut down to the ground, you who weakened the nations! For you have said in your heart: 'I will ascend into heaven, I will exalt my throne above the stars of God; I will also sit on the mount of the congregation on the farthest sides of the north; I will ascend above the heights of the clouds, I will be like the Most High." Yet you shall be brought down to Sheol, to the lowest depths of the pit.

In Revelation 12:7-9:

> And war broke out in heaven: Michael and his angels fought against the dragon; and the dragon and his angels fought, but they did not prevail, nor was a place found for them in heaven any longer. So the great dragon was cast out, that serpent of old, called the Devil and Satan, who deceives the whole

world: he was cast to the earth, and his angels were cast out with him.

Also in 2 Corinthians 11:14-15:

> For such are false apostles, deceitful workers, transforming themselves into apostles of Christ. And no wonder! For Satan himself transforms himself into an angel of light. Therefore it is no great thing if his ministers also transform themselves into ministers of righteousness, whose end will be according to their works.

Satan's role with humanity is astounding. He's like a Chess champion adjusting his pawn, j'adoube, in order to take advantage of a back-rank weakness. In the Garden of Eden, Satan offered to Eve what God had forbidden, saying not to worry, they would not die if they ate of the fruit of the tree of knowledge of good and evil. Furthermore, he told Eve that by eating the forbidden fruit, their eyes would be opened and they would be like God, knowing good and evil.

<u>Not-So-Fast</u> – 10:00 pm: Now, hold everything. Why exactly were they to die, as God had put it, if they disobeyed?

<u>Brother Carviss</u> – 10:04 pm: The prophet Isaiah helps us understand it: "Behold, the Lord's hand is not shortened, that it cannot save; nor His ear heavy, that it cannot hear. But your iniquities have separated you from your God; and your sins have hidden His face from you, so that He will not hear" (Isaiah 59:1-2).

You see, Hector, when a separation occurs, it is man who turns his back on God. Sin is the only reason this separation could occur. Unbelief is an often overlooked sin that cuts us off from the warmth of Father God's embrace.

Satan knew God had placed Adam and Eve, created flawlessly, into a perfect environment. He approached Eve and contradicted the Word of God, telling her that she surely would not die if she ate this beautiful fruit. Eve did not understand that it was the perfection of her innocence that would die: that her spirit would be opened not only to God (for good), but also to Satan (for evil). Of course, Satan was diabolically pleased to have plotted the fall of humans, because now he could communicate with them, tempt them, and actually be on their choice list for every decision they would make. This also meant that Satan, separated from God, could repeatedly lie to the human race and try to persuade them to join him in spirit.

Fast forward through the years of time, to view the many examples God has shown of humans connecting with multiple gods and higher voices, coming into that oneness with Satan. Here are only a few references to show this corroboration. (Deuteronomy 18:9-12; 2 Chronicles 33:1-6; 1 Samuel 28:7-10; 1 Kings 18:19, 25, 26; Acts 8:18-22) Today, in our age of the New Spirituality, we see such a dichotomy of language for spiritual concepts: same word or phrase, but totally different meaning. Examples of this semantics display are provided in several "Sleight of Hand" vocabulary discussions throughout coming chapters.

If the spirits of humans on earth (who believe they are little gods) and the spirits of the antichrists can mystically be fused as one, then Satan will have accomplished his eternal goal to "be like God." Recorded from Hubbard's "Christ" in *The Revelation*, is this explanation: "It is essential at the moment of infusion of empathy that you overcome all fear of separation from God. This overcoming of fear in a whole planetary experience is an irresistible force. No being can resist it" (244-245).

<u>Laurie</u> – 10:15 pm: More on the "illusion" of separation: "Your triumph over Satan, that is, over the illusion of separation, will be a victory for the universal community" (Hubbard, Revelation, op. cit. 193). According to the illusion of separation theory, some people will see a separation between God and man. It follows that the victory for the universal community will be when all people left on earth are

perceiving "love and oneness" (all are a part of God, and therefore they believe they are God). Conversely, the perception of "separate and fear" is the belief that sin separates a person from God until he/she fears the result of this separation enough to surrender to God and receive forgiveness of sins and salvation through the blood atonement of Jesus Christ. Satan is author of the "love and oneness" plan because he is a created being, and if he is a part of God and God is in him, then the victory is complete for Satan to be "like God," and therefore worthy of worship as deity.

Not-So-Fast – 10:24 pm: What about the humans who refuse to take part in this fusion, choosing to remain faithful to who they believe is the only true King of Kings and Lord of Lords?

Laurie – 10:27 pm: These humans will need to be terminated if they will not "see the light" and join the New Spirituality. The ultimate surprise, however, is that these people who believe in the fear of the Lord and that God is indeed separate (on a higher spiritual plane) from us, as humans, will be taken to heaven to live with God (in the twinkling of an eye), and will come back to earth with Christ to reign with Him!

Hector, if you, yourself, find that you have been duped by this deception, are you willing to be "pulled from the fire?"

Jude said:

> But you, beloved, building yourselves up on your most holy faith, praying in the Holy Spirit, keep yourselves in the love of God, looking for the mercy of our Lord Jesus Christ unto eternal life. And on some have compassion, making a distinction; but others save with fear, pulling them out of the fire, hating even the garment defiled by the flesh (Jude 20-23).

.Brother Carviss – 11:06 pm: Your discussion leaves me looking forward to our next session. On September 13th at 8:00 pm, we'll look at "New Revelation and New Spirituality." Here's where we'll get into more detail of what the New Age teachings are and how they have evolved. I'm grateful to Laurie and Hannah who have volunteered to prepare our "Sleight-Of-Hand" vocabulary terms each week. Next session's vocabulary words are: "The Church," "In the 'Twinkling of an Eye,'" "Adding and/or Subtracting from the Bible's Book of Revelation," "Judgment of the Quick and the Dead," and "Cast Into the Lake of Fire/The Second Death," Any other bloggers are welcome to add quotations you may find to go along with these terms. Warren Smith's *False Christ Coming. Does Anybody Care?* and the *Holy Bible* will be our main books of reference.

Until next week, September 13th at 8:00 pm,

Meryl Carviss (blog host)

@chapter_seven

THE NEW REVELATION AND NEW SPIRITUALITY

"Let all the earth fear the Lord; Let all the inhabitants of the world stand in awe of Him. For He spoke, and it was done; He commanded, and it stood fast."   (Psalm 33:8-9)

September 13, 2011 - STUDY FORUM BLOGGERS CHECKED IN:

>Brother Carviss >Laurie >Hannah "Campus-Joy" >Hector "Not-So-Fast" >Will "Square-Away"

<u>Brother Carviss</u> — 8:00 pm: Ready to blog? Tonight we're delving into some of the background and postulates regarding the New Age/New Spirituality. Much of what we'll discuss this evening can be referenced to Warren Smith's book, False *Christ Coming. Does Anybody Care?* Hold on to the reins: this promises to be quite a ride!

<u>Square-Away</u> — 8:04 pm: I'm very thankful that I know the Holy Spirit is the faithful rudder for my ship! When I think about the deception coming upon us like a tsunami at midnight, I know my anchor holds, and in Him I will rest and trust! I actually did a good bit of research on the New Revelation for this session. I'd like to share what I've found, although I'll confess that this information leaves me gasping for the clean air of the Word of God.

In 1966, Barbara Marx Hubbard, a "futurist" and "conscious evolutionist" fell into a dreamlike state and was given an intense vision of the future. This vision was reportedly in response to two questions that Barbara had directed to God: "What is our story? What in our age is comparable to the birth of Christ" (qtd. in Smith, False op. cit. 25).

Hubbard then was made to see that the earth is a living body and that humans are cells within the body of earth. She saw further into the future and noticed that the earth was now surrounded by a radiant light. Watching as the whole planet was "aligned" in "a magnetic field of love," she saw the earth lifted above the bright light. All of a sudden, Hubbard saw that people experienced a merging of their own "inner lights," while tremendous "force" emanating from the light sent powerful currents of joyful energy throughout the body of humanity. The whole world celebrated this event as the earth was "born again" (Smith, False op. cit. 25).

As time passed, Hubbard heard regularly from this "inner voice," who was telling her to go out and tell the story of "our birth." One interesting message from her "inner voice:"

> Have utter faith in my design. Achieve deep peace. Be prepared for a great force to enter your life to do this work. It cannot enter till you have achieved deep peace. Your reward for peace, which can only be achieved by faith, is contact with the great force and with the other forces waiting in the wings (Hubbard, The Revelation, op. cit., 55).

Not-So-Fast – 8:15 pm: Now we're talking! I'm up for the "other forces waiting in the wings." We're hooked up with a healthy curiosity, along with an insatiable imagination to go with it. Let's rock! This sounds better than the most tantalizing Sci Fi movie I've ever seen.

Square-Away – 8:18 pm: Hector, I know you enjoy leaning to the dark side, so try to keep an open mind. This observation into spiritual powers is not Sci Fi; rather we're glimpsing the forces of evil, often veiled in an array of pseudo-light. Here's God's Word on the issue:

- Ephesians 6:12 – "For we do no wrestle against flesh and blood, but against principalities, against powers, against the rulers of the darkness of this age, against spiritual hosts of wickedness in the heavenly places."
- 2 Corinthians 10:4-5 – "For the weapons of our warfare are not carnal but mighty in God for pulling down strongholds, casting down arguments and every high thing that exalts itself against the knowledge of God, bringing every thought into captivity to the obedience of Christ."
- 2 Corinthians 4:6 – "For it is God who commanded light to shine out of darkness who has shone in our hearts to give the light of the knowledge of the glory of God in the face of Jesus Christ. But we have this treasure in earthen vessels, that the excellence of the power may be of God and not of us."

<u>Not-So-Fast</u> – 8:29 pm: Keep going, Square-Away!

<u>Square-Away</u> – 8:32 pm: In 1979, Hubbard had a revelation that the presence in her original vision, thirteen years earlier, had been the "Christ." In 1980, Hubbard explains that in the middle of "an electrifying presence of light" her own higher self "voice" was transformed into the "Christ voice." From that point on, Hubbard received more information and direction regarding telling the world about the "planetary birth experience." Hubbard is highly respected and loved in many nations for her insights about "God," the "Christ" and the future of humanity (Smith, False, op.cit. 26).

In 1993, Hubbard wrote The *Revelation: Our Crisis Is a Birth* (later renamed *The Revelation: A Message of Hope for the New Millennium*). Hubbard and her "Christ," in many ways, rewrote the Bible's Book of Revelation. Hubbard's "Christ" discloses that if all humanity is united and purposefully partnering with God, we can actually recreate the future. For example, Hubbard's "Christ" reveals that the "violent" Armageddon of the Bible is only a "possible" future because, with more positive behavior and a total "oneness" of all humanity, we will actually see the earth make an evolutionary leap, achieving "the Planetary Birth Experience." This will usher in the "Planetary Pentecost." This "birth experience" is dependent on an "Instant of Cooperation," when humanity on earth will be mysteriously changed in "the twinkling of an eye," and we'll know what it means for humanity to be collectively born again in to a new creation (Ibid. 27-28).

As this planetary birth experience is evolving, Hubbard's "Christ" declares that all who refuse to see themselves and others as "God" and "Christ" will be removed by the "selection process." This rejected group is made up of people who hold onto "fear and separate," meaning that these people will hold fast to their biblical belief that separation (sin) does exist, and that we must receive the atonement of the blood of Jesus Christ in order to be free, forgiven, and covered with the righteousness of our Savior. Furthermore, Hubbard's "Christ" insists that those who see themselves as "separate" and not "divine" will hold back humanity's ability to evolve spiritually. Therefore, these "misfits" will go through a "selection process," which is a "purification" that will be accomplished through "the shock of a fire." The people who resist this "New Revelation" will be looked upon as "cancer cells" and must be either healed or completely removed from the body of humanity. This "selection process" will result in the deaths of those who refuse to claim their divinity. Those who fall into this rejection are looked upon as "evil" and must be "overcome" (Ibid. 28-29).

Campus-Joy – 8:45 pm: Question: How is it that those who believe in "separate" (sin) are punished by removal (death), only to be called "evil" for their belief? Does anyone else see a paradox of massive proportion here as the New Spirituality leaders indicate that all paths lead to God, and yet those who stay firmly committed to the God of the Bible, and Him alone, are facing elimination by the "selection process?"

<u>Brother Carviss</u> – 8:48 pm: These words from the apostle Paul keep coming to my mind. "Come out from among them and be separate, says the Lord. Do not touch what is unclean, and I will receive you. I will be a Father to you, and you shall be My sons and daughters, says the Lord Almighty" (2 Corinthians 6:17-18).

Thanks, Will, you've brought a lot to the table. Now we'll take a look at the "Sleight-Of-Hand" vocabulary for this week.

<u>Laurie</u> – 8:52 pm: Our first vocabulary term is "The Church."

"You were born to be me [the 'Christ']. You were born to be partners with God" (Hubbard, op. cit. 148).

"The church is the body of believers who are conscious of being me [the 'Christ']" (Hubbard, op. cit. 102).

<u>Campus-Joy</u> – 8:57 pm: "The Church"

> And Simon Peter answered and said, "You are the Christ, the Son of the living God." Jesus answered and said to him, "Blessed are you, Simon Bar-Jonah, for flesh and blood has not revealed this to you, but My Father who is in heaven. And I also say to you that you are Peter [small stone], and on this rock [boulder] I will build My church, and the gates of Hades shall not prevail against it" (Matthew 16:16-18).

<u>Laurie</u> – 9:03 pm: "In the Twinkling of an Eye"

"This universal link-up with the 'Force' results in all humanity being resurrected – lifted up and born again into a whole new way of being. In the twinkling of an eye, they are taken to a new spiritual level as they now actually experience themselves as a part of God" (Smith, False, op. cit. 98).

Campus-Joy – 9:06 pm: "In the Twinkling of an Eye"

> For the Lord Himself will descend from heaven with a shout, with the voice of an archangel, and with the trumpet of God. And the dead in Christ will rise first. Then we who are alive and remain shall be caught up together with them in the clouds to meet the Lord in the air. And thus we shall always be with the Lord (1 Thessalonians 4:16-17).
>
> Behold, I tell you a mystery: We shall not all sleep, but we shall all be changed – in a moment, in the twinkling of an eye, at the last trumpet. For the trumpet will sound and the dead will be raised incorruptible, and we shall be changed. For this corruptible must put on incorruption, and this mortal must put on immortality (1 Corinthians 15:51-53).

Laurie - 9:13 pm: "Adding and/or Subtracting from the Bible's Book of Revelation"

"This text was written not to add or subtract from the divine book of Revelation. It was written to inform you of the alternative to Armageddon" (Hubbard, op. cit. 305).

Campus-Joy – 9:16 pm: "Adding and/or Subtracting from the Bible's Book of Revelation"

> For I testify to everyone who hears the words of the prophecy of this book: If anyone adds to these things, God will add to him the plagues that are written in this book; and if anyone takes away from the words of the book of this prophecy, God shall take away his part from the Book of Life, from the holy city, and from the things which are written in this book (Revelation 22: 18-19).

Laurie – 9:21 pm: "Judgment of the Quick and the Dead"

"The decisive moment of selection has almost come. The judgment of the quick and the dead is about to be made. The end of this phase of evolution is nearly complete" (Hubbard, Revelation 189).

"At the time of the Quantum Instant there will be a judgment of the quick and the dead. That is, there will be an evolutionary selection process based on your qualifications for co-creative power" (Ibid. 102).

Campus-Joy – 9:25 pm: "Judgment of the Quick and the Dead"

"I charge you, therefore before God and the Lord Jesus Christ, who will judge the living and the dead at His appearing and His kingdom: Preach the Word! Be ready in season and out of season. Convince, rebuke, exhort, with all longsuffering and teaching" (2 Timothy 4:1-2).

Laurie – 9:30 pm: "Cast into the Lake of Fire/The Second Death"

> Cynics, disbelievers, those who fear and cannot love: know that the mercy of God almighty is with you now. The second death, for you, is a purification, an erasing of the memory of fear, through the shock of a fire. It will burn out the imprint upon your soul that is blocking you from seeing the glory which shall be revealed in you (Hubbard, op. cit. 267).

Campus-Joy – 9:34 pm: "Cast into the Lake of Fire/The Second Death"

> Then the beast was captured, and with him the false prophet who worked signs in his presence, by which he deceived those who received the mark of the beast and those who worshiped his image. These two were cast alive into the lake of fire burning with brimstone (Revelation 19:20).

Brother Carviss – 9:39: "New Age/New Spirituality" packaging has morphed into just the simple term, "New Spirituality," which is considerably less offensive to an unsuspecting audience. The "New Spirituality" must be comprehended as most ancient. From the beginning, we must be acutely aware of the enemy of our souls, Lucifer, the once exalted brightest of the angels. We should pray for discernment and wisdom for this time in which we live. At the same time, we ought to become wise as serpents and harmless as doves. "Why?"

Here's one good reason:

New Age leaders declare that terrorism is not a result of what people do. Rather, it is a result of how people think and believe. Therefore, terrorism is a spiritual problem, necessitating a spiritual solution. The startling discovery is that, hidden within this fast-paced New Age/New Gospel Peace Plan, complete with the promises of safety, peace and love for those who comply, is the "selection process," prepared to re-educate or eliminate biblical Christianity and all of its followers (Smith, False op. cit. 9).

Paul, the apostle, in 2 Corinthians 1:1-4, warned the believers in Corinth not to be deceived by a false Christ, or by a false Holy Spirit, or by a gospel that does not follow the tenants of the true biblical Gospel. Many warnings go out to believers, admonishing them not to be deceived by spiritual experiences and teachings that are not from God. Jesus even warned his disciples, specifically, that spiritual deception would be a sign of the end of times.

Smith reflects on his experience as a former New Ager, and is dismayed that so many believers are:

-falling under the power of the same New Age spirit;

-listening to a spirit that advises we need breakthroughs for the fulfillment of our destiny;

-submitting to a spirit who says there's something new, a transition, a paradigm shift;

-looking for a new revelation and personal experience that will take the church to further dimensions toward a whole new level (Smith, False, op. cit. 12).

<u>Laurie</u> – 9:55 pm: These "new teachings" are actually ancient, practiced by the "desert fathers" as far back as the third century. The current purpose is to unify the world's religions in order to bring world peace. "The Christ" of the New Spirituality proclaims that humanity has forgotten who they are. The "new paradigm" explains that humanity is not made of sinners, not separate from God, and not needing a Savior. Rather, every human is part of God and God is part of each human. Salvation is collective as we all accept this universal notion and realize that oneness and love are the only requirements, while fear and separation are the only hindrances to this salvation (Ibid. 13).

Enter: Helen Schucman and Marianne Williamson. In 1965, Helen Schucman, a Columbia University Professor of Medical Psychology, began a seven and a half year trek in journaling what her "inner voice" was expounding: *A Course in Miracles*. Alarmingly, Schucman's "Jesus" taught a totally different gospel than the gospel of the Bible. Ironically, Schucman used Christian terms, along with alluring psychology, to persuade readers to accept that love is all there is, and any illusion of fear or sin or a Devil is to be corrected. *The Course* also teaches that "the Christ" is in everyone and that "the Christ" is humanity's divine connection with God and with one another. Wrong thinking, according to *The Course in Miracles*, has led to the misperception that humans are sinners and need an external Christ to save them. This notion makes meaningless the "slain Christ," and therefore the cross is not needed for salvation. The *Course* touts the "Atonement" ("at-one-ment") as the means of salvation. Of course, you must understand that "Atonement" in the *Course* means remembering and affirming each person's "oneness" (at-one-ment) with God and with creation (Ibid. 17-19).

In 1992, Marianne Williamson wrote *A Return to Love: Reflections on the Principles of A Course in Miracles*. Williamson's book was featured on *The Oprah Winfrey Show*. Following Oprah's endorsement, *Reflections* found itself at the top of *The New York Times* best-seller list. Ministers who tended to follow the trend, joined Robert Schuler in marketing *A Course in Miracles* by teaching these principles in seminars and from their pulpits. Williamson, in her 1997 book, *Healing the Soul of America*, was able to advance the "New Spirituality" doctrine to include the political arena. Soon Williamson was able to collaborate with author, Neale Donald Walsch, to co-found The Global Renaissance Alliance. A member of the Alliance's board, Barbara Marx Hubbard, soon appeared on the scene with on-going "new revelation" obtained from her "inner voice," claiming to be "the Christ" (Ibid. 20).

It is anticipated that Alliance members will be a significant presence during future crises. Because they believe that "their Christ" has a plan to save the world from destruction, they will persistently introduce the New Age/New Spirituality Peace Plan which "their Christ" has described as the "alternative to Armageddon" (Ibid. 99).

<u>Brother Carviss</u> – 10:14 pm: There is much to ponder, much to question, much to put to prayer as we expose the rudiments of the spiritual paradigm shift that is swiftly progressing on our planet! It is well time for the Church of our Lord and Savior Jesus Christ to wake up, pray up, stand up, and speak up. Paul, in writing to the church at Thessalonica, warned, "The coming of the lawless one is according to the working of Satan, with all power, signs, and lying wonders, and with all unrighteous deception among those who perish, because they did not receive the love of the truth, that they might be saved" (2 Thessalonians 2:9-10). Could it be possible for these lying wonders to

be received as a much sought-after breakthrough and "end times revival" in the church? How can that depth of deception be avoided?

<u>Laurie</u> — 10:20 pm: I'd suggest we "receive the love of the truth" of which Paul wrote by asking our Father for discernment and for wisdom in testing the spirits to see if they are of God Almighty! "Beloved, do not believe every spirit, but test the spirits, whether they are of God; because many false prophets have gone out into the world" (1 John 4:1).

<u>Campus-Joy</u> — 10:25 pm: My friends and I are always talking about all of this. Sometimes, we split up and visit the menagerie of religious groups meeting on campus, then we meet up to share and discuss what we've seen. Strangely, many of the DUPED concerns are the very issues we're detecting on our campus blog, but the campus language is definitely vaguer and less threatening. I find that interesting and puzzling.

<u>Brother Carviss</u> — 10:29 pm: Allow me to respond to your observation, Hannah, by quoting Warren Smith:

> The "Armageddon Alternative" Peace Plan has been given by the false New Age "Christ" to his "avant-garde" channelers who are now in the process of gradually introducing this plan, with its underlying New Age principles, to an unsuspecting general public. But the "Armageddon Alternative" is not referred to as such at this time. The terms and concepts are presented in simple sound bites about the virtues of "love," "peace," and "oneness," while warning about the dangers of "fear," "hate," "self-centeredness," and "separation" Because things are being kept purposefully vague, there is no open talk about the plan's "selection process." At least not yet (Smith. False, op. cit. 96).

<u>Square-Away</u> — 10:35 pm: Using my familiar "nautical noggin," it all seems pretty hopeless. However, I will always choose to stand on the

side of my Lord and know that He will guide me by His Holy Spirit's direction. When necessary, He'll give me the strength to "run against a troop and leap over a wall" (2 Samuel 22:30)! All that I could ever need to sail on the high seas of tumult, my God will supply. So, I ask you, what do I have to fear? Nothing!

Not-So-Fast – 10:39 pm: Why do I feel so ambivalent, not choosing either side as to where I'll stand? My normal response is that "all is bunk in the religious realm." Now, somehow that hiding place seems exposed and worthless.

Square-Away – 10:43 pm: Hang in here, Hector. The important thing is that you are staying open and considering what you're hearing with fresh perspective.

Brother Carviss – 10:45 pm: One thing for sure: when anyone now approaches us regarding a "collective salvation," we'll know what they mean. We will also have an answer for the hope that lies within us of the exclusive salvation of Jesus Christ, the son of the living God.

It's been an informative, yet heavy session. As always, I thank you for your preparation and participation. Next week, we'll take a look at how easy it is for people, especially Christians, to become involved in this New Spirituality. We'll be using Richard Foster's book, *Celebration of Discipline*, a forerunner to his 1992 work, *Prayer: Finding the Heart's True Home*. In the latter book, Foster gives credence to various "mystics" and "church fathers" who have evidenced this work of contemplative prayer in their lives: Clement of Alexanadria, Isaac of Nineveh, dessert father – Ammonas, Madame Guyon, Bernard of Clairvaux, and Teresa of Avila. Foster takes us through various steps into contemplative prayer, including: (1) Recollection, also called "centering prayer," "prayer of presence," and "centering down;" (2) The prayer of Quiet; (3) Spiritual Ecstasy, including out-of-body experiences. Foster also gives caution that the new Christian should not try this type of prayer because of the possibility of engaging supernatural guidance that is not divine. He gives examples of "prayers of protection" that could be used by Christians before entering into contemplative prayer (Foster, Prayer 155-165).

Our "Sleight-Of-Hand" vocabulary for next week will include the terms, "Born Again," "Accepting Christ," "Atonement," "The Name of Christ," "Salvation," and "Having the Mind of Christ." Next week, we'll give Hannah and Laurie a little break, as all of us prepare to share in the vocabulary.

Until next week, September 20th at 8:00 pm,

Meryl Carviss (blog host)

@chapter_eight

TO MEDITATE OR NOT TO MEDITATE

> "...If you abide in My word, you are My disciples indeed. And you shall know the truth, and the truth shall make you free." (John 8:31-32)

September 20, 2011 – STUDY FORUM BLOGGERS CHECKED IN:

>Brother Carviss >Laurie >Hannah "Campus-Joy" >Hector "Not-so-Fast" >Will "Square-Away"

<u>Brother Carviss</u> - 8:00 pm: Happy First Week of Autumn, Bloggers! Thanks for your research on this week's topic: "To Meditate or Not to Meditate." Of course, we know that the topic this week will include not only meditation, but also *Celebration of Discipline*, Richard Foster's work on spiritual formation and contemplative prayer. To begin, let's warm up with what we've found in the "Sleight-Of-Hand" vocabulary for this session. We'll explore the terms: "Born again," "Accepting Christ," "Atonement," "The name of Christ," "Salvation," and "Having the mind of Christ." I'll begin:

I'm looking at the term, "Born Again," from Hubbard's "Christ" in her book: *The Revelation:*

> The selection process will exclude all who are exclusive. The selection process assures that only the loving will evolve to the stage of co-creator ... After the selection process, you will be born to the next stage of evolution. There will be a new

heaven, a new earth, a new body and a new consciousness for all who survive (Hubbard, op. cit.33-34).

It is important to note that Hubbard's term concerning a new birth is not the same as the Bible's use of the term, "born again."

<u>Not-So-Fast</u> – 8:10 pm: Hold on now, just exactly how would a person be born again? One can't go back to conception and start all over again!

<u>Laurie</u> – 8:13 pm: Oh, thanks, Hector, you've set this up perfectly! An intelligent skeptic, much like you, sneaked in to see Jesus at night. Nicodemus, a teacher of Israel, asked Jesus that very same question.

> Jesus answered and said to him, "Most assuredly, I say to you, unless one is born again, he cannot see the kingdom of God."
>
> Nicodemus said to Him, "How can a man be born when he is old? Can he enter a second time into his mother's womb and be born?"
>
> Jesus answered, "Most assuredly, I say to you, unless one is born of water and the Spirit, he cannot enter the kingdom of God. That which is born of the flesh is flesh, and that which is born of the Spirit is spirit" (John 3: 3-6).

<u>Not-So-Fast</u> – 8:16 pm: I still don't get it, but I believe I'd like to.

<u>Laurie</u> – 8:18 pm: Ok, then, we'll move down, just a few verses, in John 3, and read what is probably the most quoted verse in the entire Bible. "For God so loved the world that He gave His only begotten Son, that whoever believes in Him should not perish but have everlasting life" (John 3:16).

<u>Not-So-Fast</u> – 8:23 pm: Don't get too excited now, but I think this is the time that I should really begin listening to what the Bible has to say. All this New Revelation, New Spirituality stuff is freaking me out just a bit. You can all laugh now!

Brother Carviss – 8:26: Trust us, Hector, nobody's laughing! Just stop and ask questions any time. Now, let's move to a similar topic, "Accepting Christ." Who'd like to jump in?

Square-Away – 8:30: "Jump in" must be my cue! I found an oddly interesting quote from Williamson's *A Return to Love: Reflections on the Principles of A Course in Miracles*. Listen to this: "We are holy beings, individual cells in the body of Christ … We are who God created us to be. We are all one, we are love itself. 'Accepting the Christ' is merely a shift in self-perception" (op. cit.32).

Listen, I couldn't swallow that one, so I quickly found help from the Bible. The apostle Paul reminds us: "For He [Father God] made Him [Jesus Christ] who knew no sin to be sin for us, that we might become the righteousness of God in Him [Jesus Christ]" (2 Corinthians 5:21). So, I can now explain that accepting Christ is the decision a person makes when he/she confesses sin, knowing that Christ became sin for us so that we could become His righteousness. Then, we accept Christ as Savior and Lord.

Not-So-Fast – 8:34 pm: Well, I found a quotation about atonement, but it is confusing, especially in the light of what has just been given. The quotation is from Schucman's writing, *A Course in Miracles*. "The full awareness of the Atonement, then, is the recognition that the separation never occurred. The Atonement is the final lesson he [man] need learn, for it teaches him that, never having sinned, he has no need of salvation" (qtd. in Smith, op. cit. 22).

Campus-Joy – 8:41: Hector, the separation that Will biblically quoted means the pulling away from God that happens when we choose to live a life in sin rather than living in God's presence of forgiveness and grace. In the New Spirituality, however, you just read that the atonement means to accept the belief that separation (or sin) never occurred. Therefore, these people believe that there was never a need for a Savior! In the Bible book of Romans we read, "For if, when we were enemies, we were reconciled to God by the death of His Son, much more, being reconciled, we shall be saved by His life. And not only so, but we also joy in God through our Lord Jesus Christ, by whom we have now received the atonement" (Romans 5:10-11). Hector, even though these times are riddled with ambiguity and delusion, there has actually never been a time when the deadly differences between God's way and man's way (more correctly, Satan's way) have been clearer.

Not-So-Fast – 8:48 pm: I hear these phrases: "Born again," "Having the mind of Christ," "Power in the name of Christ," and "Salvation" (among others). I've always had an argument, opposite from Christians, for each of these terms. Now, I am beginning to see the fallacy in the stance I've taken in the New Spirituality, yet I don't fully understand the foundation in the Bible either.

Campus-Joy – 8:52 pm: Hector, you're moving so close to an understanding of Holy Scripture. Just keep moving with us as we discuss the term, "The name of Christ." First of all, again from Schucman's writing: *A Course in Miracles*, we read, "Is He [Jesus] the Christ? O yes, along with you. The name of Jesus Christ, as such, is but a symbol that is safely used as a replacement for the many names of all the gods to which you pray" (qtd. in Smith, op. cit. 21).

Yet, in the Holy Bible, we see the ultimate power that resides in the Name of Christ:

> Therefore God also has highly exalted Him and given Him the name which is above every name, that at the name of Jesus every knee should bow, of those in heaven and of those on earth, and of those under the earth, and that every tongue should confess that Jesus is Lord, to the glory of God the Father (Philippians 2:9-10).

Brother Carviss – 8:59 pm: It's tragic that so many people have been duped by the confusion of terms and their meanings. The New Spirituality uses terms found in God's Word, but their terms have totally different meanings. Hector, I hope this difference in the meaning of "Salvation" will be clear to you. Warren Smith in his book, *False Christ Coming: Does Anybody Care?* shows the erroneous New Age belief about its "reinvented" Christ:

> We are not "sinners" separate from God. We are all part of the one body of Christ and the one body of God. Salvation does not come by grace from accepting Jesus Christ as the Son of God. Rather it is achieved – when we accept ourselves as Christ and when we accept ourselves as God. The New Age Gospel teaches that when humanity collectively accepts and experiences itself as being a part of Christ and a part of God, we will not only save ourselves, we will save our world (Smith, False, op. cit. 13).

Now, Hector, this time hear the Word of the Lord:

> If we this day are judged for a good deed done to the helpless man, by what means he has been made well, let it be known to you all, and to all the people of Israel, that by the name of Jesus Christ of Nazareth, whom you crucified, whom God raised from the dead, by Him this man stands here before you whole. This was the "stone which was rejected by you builders, which has become the chief cornerstone." Nor is there salvation in any other, for there is no other name under heaven given among men by which we must be saved (Acts 4:9-12).

Not-So-Fast – 9:10 pm: On first impulse, I'd say I'm very confused, but in reality I'm sensing that for the very first time, confusion is being scattered. The Word of God is becoming clear to me as it relates to Jesus Christ of the Bible. I actually think I'd better start reading that Bible, especially as much as I've harassed and attempted to douse your faith with doubt!

<u>Campus-Joy</u>: 9:13 pm: Our last term for this week's "Sleight-of-Hand" vocabulary is, "Having the mind of Christ." This is particularly thought-provoking to me since I am a college student and very aware of what my mind absorbs. From Williamson's work, *A Return To Love: Reflections on the Principles of A Course in Miracles*, "The concept of a divine, or 'Christ' mind, is the idea that, at our core, we are not just identical, but actually the same being. 'There is only one begotten Son' doesn't mean that someone else was it, and we're not. It means we're all it. There's only one of us here" (op. cit. 30-31).

There's a group from my Spiritual Formation class at school which meets on Sunday evenings to meditate and spend time in The Silence. They've even built a labyrinth on campus, and they use it to go into deeper places with God. I'm not sure what all of that means, but I've not sensed a "green light" to attend those Sunday meetings. I've heard my classmates talk about the "oneness" and that atonement really means "at-one-ment." Somehow, the quote I just gave seems vaguely familiar, and it is not a comfortable feeling that I have.

<u>Brother Carviss</u> – 9:22 pm: I'm so thankful that the prospect of your going to those "oneness" meetings is not comfortable to you. The themes of meditation and contemplative prayer are what we'll discuss in today's main study! Before that, let's look at the Bible's explanation of "Having the mind of Christ:"

> Let this mind be in you which was also in Christ Jesus, who, being in the form of God, did not consider it robbery to be equal with God, but made Himself of no reputation, taking the form of a servant and coming in the likeness of men. And being found in appearance as a man, He humbled Himself and became obedient to the point of death, even the death of the cross (Romans 5:10-11).

Well, this is quite a contrasting view as compared to Ms Williamson's work in *A Return To Love: Reflections on the Principles of A Course in Miracles!* Aren't we thankful that God has watched over His Word through all these centuries, and that we can know His truth on which to stand?

Now, on to the topic for today – "To Meditate Or Not To Meditate." To begin, I would quickly agree that all Christians are involved in spiritual formation. That is, if we're alive, we are engaged in movement and growth as Father God conforms us ever closer to the image of His son, Jesus Christ. Also, spiritual formation requires certain spiritual disciplines in order to accommodate this growth. We learn about these disciplines, such as prayer, study, meditation of God's Word, etc. as we move through our life with Christ.

The problem I want to highlight today, however, is the introduction of meditation and contemplative prayer as experiential visits into the spirit world, a place where prayers for protection are advised. As I have researched this topic, I've found that thousands and thousands of evangelical Christians and their leaders are entering deeply into spiritual formation, using meditation and contemplative prayer to delve deeply into the spirit world. Entire protestant denominations are affirming these practices and teaching them in Christian colleges, universities, and seminaries. What an effective way to infiltrate hundreds of churches: send out class after class of seminary graduates, ordained with extensive training in obtaining mantra meditation and contemplative prayer! I mention protestants, in particular, because the Catholic church has been using these devices for hundreds of years, in the solitary environment of the desert and in monasteries, among other places.

It becomes apparent that a common thread of the current trend in meditation and contemplative prayer is a much loved book, written in 1978, by Richard Foster: *Celebration of Discipline*. How shocking to read the background and methods highlighted in Foster's hallmark book to explain the New Spirituality. Foster lists writers who have purported this new way:

Christian writers throughout the centuries have spoken of a way of listening to God, of communing with the Creator of heaven and earth, of experiencing the Eternal Lover of the world. Such fine thinkers as Augustine, Francis of Assisi, Francois Fenelon, Madame Guyon, Bernard of Clairvaux, Francis de Sales, Juliana of Norwich, Brother Lawrence, George Fox, John Woolman, Evelyn Underhill, Thomas Merton, Frank Laubach, Thomas Kelly and many others speak of this more excellent way (Foster, Celebration 14).

A visit to your favorite search engine will disclose the common beliefs of these writers.

Campus-Joy – 9:45 pm: This is really hitting home with me. Richard Foster's book, *Celebration of Discipline* was the first of our assigned readings for my Spiritual Formation course this semester. I would like to share more about "The Silence" which Foster promotes.

Foster encourages his readers to move beyond the superficial religious culture and to go down in recreating silences, and into the inner world of contemplation. The masters of meditation report exciting possibilities for new life and freedom, as well as adventures into the unexplored inner regions of the frontier of the spirit. Mr. Foster asserts that it is a sad commentary that our young people must turn to Zen, Yoga, or Transcendental Meditation (TM) since modern Christianity has failed in courage to train its youth to explore the ancient, yet contemporary, art of meditation and contemplative prayer (Ibid., op. cit. 14-15).

Square-Away – 9:51 pm: Does it strike any of you as strange that our youth should be fed a rich diet of meditation and exploration of the spirit world so they won't turn to Zen, Yoga, or TM? Would we give our kids cocaine so they will be satisfied and won't buy it from drug dealers? I may just be a nature-lovin' fisherman, but I have more common sense and good old discernment than that!

<u>Brother Carviss</u> – 9:57 pm: Yes, Hannah's last contribution strikes me as, not only strange, but highly concerning!

As we look further into Foster's work, we'll introduce two types of meditation. First, and what is referenced multiple times in the Bible, is the practice of reading, thinking, reasoning, and exalting the Word of God. Second, is an ancient-future style of meditation, which uses such practices as "mantra meditation," "centering down," "palms up/palms down," "breathing techniques," and the tremendous "power of imagination," leading seekers to empty their minds in order to fill their minds with the communication received during their meeting in the spirit world (Ibid., op. cit. 24-25).

<u>Laurie</u> – 10:04 pm: You can believe that I am disappointed and alarmed at what we're sharing. I noticed on page 22 of *Celebration of Discipline*, Foster highlights the imagination as the easiest way to enter the inner world of meditation. He emphasizes that the human imagination is more powerful than conceptual thought and stronger than the human will (Ibid., op. cit. 22). Is this perhaps why the Holy Scriptures cite this power of imagination as something to be cast down in spiritual warfare? "For the weapons of our warfare are not carnal, but mighty in God for pulling down strongholds; casting down arguments [imaginations], and every high thing that exalts itself against the knowledge of God, bringing every thought into captivity to the obedience of Christ ..." (2 Corinthians 10:4-5).

In coordination with imaginations being the easiest way to enter the inner world of meditation, I found in Foster's *Celebration of Discipline* an explanation of the key part dreams play.

In speaking of dreams as being a key to unlocking the inner world door, Foster specifies that it is wise to pray a prayer of protection, because opening ourselves to spiritual influence can be dangerous as well as profitable. He instructs us to ask God to surround us with His light of protection as He ministers to our spirit (Foster, Celebration op. cit. 23).

Question: If we're actually entering the spirit world, and therefore need defended, then how do we know that this "light of protection" for which we're asking is not the "angel of light" as spoken of in the Bible? "… For Satan himself transforms himself into an angel of light. Therefore it is no great thing if his ministers also transform themselves into ministers of righteousness, whose end will be according to their works" (2 Corinthians 11:14-15).

Now, here's a thought: Satan comes forth as an angel of light with Christians in order to not "blow his cover." The strategy is to convince Christians that the feeling of joy and euphoria is from the Holy Spirit --- especially when Satan quotes a timely delivered scripture to them. The idea is to build up trust in the "inner voice," as Christians receive specific advice tailored to their personal lives.

<u>Campus-Joy</u> – 10:14 pm: I'd like to share what I got from *Celebration of Discipline*, where "out of body experiences" were discussed. I'll do a direct quotation on this discipline:

> After awhile there is a deep yearning within to go into the upper regions beyond the clouds. In your imagination allow your spiritual body, shining with light, to rise out of your physical body. Look back so that you can see yourself lying in the grass and reassure your body that you will return momentarily. Imagine your spiritual self, alive and vibrant, rising up through the clouds and into the stratosphere. Observe your physical body, the knoll, and the forest shrink as you leave the earth. Go deeper and deeper into outer space until there is nothing except the warm presence of the eternal Creator. Rest in His presence. Listen quietly, anticipating the unanticipated. Note carefully any instruction given …When it is time for you to leave, audibly thank the Lord for His goodness and return to the meadow. … (Foster, Celebration, op. cit. 27-28).

This is so frightening to me! It makes me think of a book I read last summer, before beginning college at Belleview Christian. The book is entitled *Castles in the Sand*. Many concepts we've discussed on this blog were actually presented as happening in this work of fiction. I remember the words that made me think of this "out of body experience." An old text was being quoted. It was from an autobiography of Teresa of Avila:

> You feel and see yourself carried away, you know not whither....Occasionally I was able, by great effort, to make a slight resistance; but afterward I was worn out, like a person who had been contending with a strong giant; at other times it was impossible to resist at all: my soul was carried away, and almost always my head with it,------I had no power over it,------and now and then the whole body as well, so that it was lifted up from the ground (qtd. from C. Greene 74).

<u>Square- Away</u> – 10:20 pm: Ok, now, hold that call! I have some questions:

- Where in the Bible do we read instructions about learning to meditate in order to enter the spirit world of both good and evil spirits?
- Doesn't the Bible, in fact, warn against such exploration?
- Aren't these practices really going beyond the Bible in their context?
- What about all the Christians through the ages, and including now, who don't have a clue as to what is erroneously displayed here as biblical truth?
- How in "Sam Hill" could teachers, pastors, and professors in Christian colleges, universities, and seminaries present this spiritual meditation, giving the encouragement that one will be led into maturity as exploration is made?

It seems to me that someone will have a lot of questions to answer!

Brother Carviss – 10:23 pm: You're correct about that, Will! I almost resist giving this next example of spiritual exploration explained by Richard Foster, but I know I must. Another nugget along the pilgrimage of meditation and contemplative prayer is the "dark night of the soul." St. John of the Cross, a Spanish mystic, describes this phenomenon as an experience to be welcomed, as a sick person might welcome a needed surgery. Allegedly, the purpose of the "dark night of the soul" is to set us free. St. John of the Cross looked upon this as a divine appointment, involving a sense of dryness, depression, and a loss of emotional life. The hope is that during this time of darkness, God may work an inner transformation upon the soul. The seriousness of this venture is vividly described by St. John, stating that the sensory and spiritual appetites are put to sleep, depriving the seeker of the ability to find pleasure in anything. It binds the imagination, and makes the memory cease as the intellect becomes dark and unable to understand anything. Next, the will becomes arid, as all the faculties become empty and useless, as a burdensome cloud keeps the soul withdrawn from God (Foster, Celebration, op. cit. 89-90).

Remember, the goal of this experience is to be set free. Do you wonder which "god" is orchestrating this darkness?

Laurie – 10:29 pm: You know, much has been made, and continues to be made, of Richard Foster's best seller, *Celebration of Discipline*. Many evangelical colleges, universities, and seminaries have used this book, as required reading, since its publishing in 1978. Thirty years later, Foster has written a new book on Spiritual Transformation: *Life With God – Reading the Bible for Spiritual Transformation*. In the latter book's chapter, "Reading with the Heart," we are introduced to the ancient practice of the Latin, *lectio divina*, which means "spiritual reading." Foster claims that *lectio divina* allows one's mind to "descend into the heart," thus accomplishing an immersion where the quieted mind allows the human spirit to engage a dynamic rendezvous with the Holy Spirit (Foster, Life 62-63).

The practice of *lectio divina* became known in the third Century, as practiced by Catholic monks. The practice is still popular among Catholics and Gnostics, and is becoming widely accepted by Christians of the "New Spirituality." *Lectio divina* is also adaptable for people of other faiths as they read their respective scriptures, while people of no faith can simply make modifications of the method to satisfy their secular beliefs, as in Transcendental Meditation (TM) (Foster, Celebrate, op. cit. 15).

Let's look to Richard Foster again to get a better handle on TM. Foster reveals that all Eastern forms of meditation require detachment, with an emphasis on losing personhood and merging with the Cosmic Mind, in a pool of cosmic consciousness. Zen and Yoga are popular forms, and TM has the same Buddhist roots. In its western form, however, TM becomes meditation for the materialist, totally separate from the spiritual realm. In this form, one is interested in controlling the brain waves to improve physiological and emotional health. More advanced TM does involve the spiritual nature, and then assumes exactly the same characteristics of all Eastern religions (Ibid.).

Campus-Joy – 10:40 pm: It's a valid question: What is the difference between biblical meditation and New Spirituality's meditation? We've just highlighted meditation of the New Spirituality. Now, let's visit some examples from God's Word. The meditation of the Bible involves conscious thought about Scripture and its application to our lives. Let's look at some examples:

"All Scripture is given by inspiration of God, and is profitable for doctrine, for reproof, for correction, for instruction in righteousness, that the man of God may be complete, thoroughly equipped for every good work" (2 Timothy 3:16-17).

" ... but his delight is in the law of the Lord, and in His law he meditates day and night" (Psalm 1:2).

"I will also meditate on all Your work, and talk of all Your deeds" (Psalm 77:12).

"This Book of the Law shall not depart from your mouth, but you shall meditate in it day and night, that you may observe to do according to all that is written in it. For then you will make your way prosperous, and then you will have good success" (Joshua 1:8).

"Oh, how I love your law! It is my meditation all the day" (Psalm 119:97).

Brother Carviss – 10:45: The peace which is experienced in biblical meditation is not found in shallow breathing or blocking out all thought in order to communicate with the spirit world. Rather, the peace of God comes as we realize the truth that God is all-powerful, and He has provided just what we need in His Word.

Further, "centering prayer" is a technique many Christians use as they try to get closer to God. Participants meditate on one word or a phrase hoping to open their hearts to communicate with God.

It is interesting to note two further paragraphs of caution, given by Richard Foster, as seekers move toward contemplative prayer:

> I also want to give a word of precaution. In the silent contemplation of God we are entering deeply into the spiritual realm, and there is such a thing as supernatural guidance that is not divine guidance. While the Bible does not give us a lot of information on the nature of the spiritual world, we do know ... there are various orders of spiritual beings, and some of them are definitely not in cooperation with God and his way! ... But for now I want to encourage you to learn and practice prayers of protection ... "All dark and evil spirits must now leave" (Foster, Prayer, op. cit. 157).

> At the onset I need to give a word of warning, a little like the warning labels on medicine bottles. Contemplative prayer is

not for the novice. I do not say this about other forms of prayer. All are welcome, regardless of proficiency or expertise, to enter freely into adoration and meditation and intercession and a host of other approaches to prayer. But contemplation is different. While we are all precious in the eyes of God, we are all not equally ready to listen to "God's speech in his wondrous, terrible, gentle, loving, all embracing silence" (Ibid. 156).

It would do us well to acknowledge that these paragraphs of caution were written by Richard Foster, himself, and not written by a critic on contemplative prayer. Also, the criteria for readiness in contemplative prayer lacks explanation. This criteria is also blatantly missing from God's Word.

This has been an intense session. Thanks for the preparation you obviously made. Next week, our blog session will be on "Interfaith Marches On." By interfaith, I mean the blending of many world religions to become that one world faith so many are promoting. How could this ever be achieved? Let's find out all we can for next week. Does anyone have another comment or question?

Not-So-Fast – 10:58 pm: As some may have noticed, I haven't made my usual sarcastic comments today. In fact, I haven't blogged much at all today. For once, I'm without words. This all sounds very surreal. Yet, I know I've heard these spirit-world terms plenty of times from my friends who are "all-in" on New Age theories. I've heard enough to know that I want to give my life to the one, true, living God that you all talk about. My life seems to be flashing before my eyes, and it's not a handsome sight! I've been proud, intolerant, unforgiving, and insolent. It's been my intention to keep people at a distance, and God even further away. I know now, with certainty, that Jesus Christ is the son of God, and that He gave His life to pay for my sin. I'm asking forgiveness for my sinful life. I'm turning away from the life I've been trudging through, and turning toward the life I've seen in you all. Brother Carviss, will you help me?

<u>Brother Carviss</u> – 11:03 pm: Hector, you indeed have figured it out! You've admitted your guilt, and acknowledged Jesus Christ as the Son of God. You've put the truth of "repentance" into your own words. Now, you just need to pray and invite the Lord Jesus Christ into your life, telling Him that you gladly receive His gift of salvation. Just talk to Father God, because He is now your Father, and you are His son! We're here to help you, Hector, as you begin your walk as a Christian. We're so happy for you, and do you know that the angels in heaven are rejoicing because of the decision you just made? We're proud of you, Brother!

Next week's topic will be: "Interfaith Marches On." Our "Sleight-Of-Hand" vocabulary terms are: "New Jerusalem," "Overcomers," "Co-creative," "Empathy," "Pentecost." Once more, we'll ask Hannah and Laurie to prepare for the vocabulary.

In order to prepare for the interfaith topic, we'll need to rely on the internet, as well as Smith's *False Christ Coming. Does Anybody Care?* Of course, our precious *Holy Bible* is our supreme resource!

Until next Tuesday, September 27, at 8:00 p.m.,

Meryl Carviss (blog host)

@chapter_nine

INTERFAITH MARCHES ON

> "'Behold the days are coming when all that is in your house, and what your fathers have accumulated until this day, shall be carried to Babylon; nothing shall be left,' says the Lord. 'And they shall take away some of your sons who will descend from you, whom you will beget; and they shall be eunuchs in the palace of the king of Babylon.' Then Hezekiah said to Isaiah, 'The word of the Lord which you have spoken is good!' For he said, 'At least there will be peace and truth in my days.'"
> (Isaiah 39: 6-8)

September 27, 2011 – STUDY FORUM BLOGGERS CHECKED IN:

\>Brother Carviss \>Laurie \>Hannah "Campus-Joy" \>Hector "Not-so-Fast" \>Will "Square-Away"

<u>Brother Carviss</u> – 8:00 pm: Hello everyone! Let's begin this session by looking back a bit:

- We began our study by noticing some strange concepts in a new movement, the emerging church.
- After reading several authors from the emerging (emergent) church, it became apparent that, while each emerging church has its own version of the "story of God," there were definitely some common threads worth pursuing.

- Surprisingly, the strange concepts and common threads were often found to have a meshing within New Age/New Spirituality goals and strategies.
- Exploring even deeper, it became all too clear that Satan, the great deceiver, was at work weaving his plan of deception to accomplish his original purpose: to be as God.
- We came to an understanding that there is a multi-leveled preparation underway to usher in a global government, with all parts globally directed, including faith-based living.

This evening's session will probe the massive and inundative Interfaith Movement, designed to envelop all world religions using common ground to bond all the willing peoples of Planet Earth. Several of our references this session will be web addresses, since the information is so current and fluid at this time. Let's begin by examining various agencies who are pulsating at a frenzied pace to provide what is needed in time for the pre-determined outcome.

According to Wikipedia, the term "interfaith" refers to positive and cooperative interaction between people of various religions, or faiths, as well as people with spiritual or humanistic beliefs. This refers to people at individual, as well as institutional status. The goal is to find a common ground in belief by focusing on similarities between faiths with an understanding of values. "Interfaith" strategies are differentiated from syncretism or alternative religion because interfaith dialogue is targeted at promoting understanding between different religions in order to increase acceptance of others, rather than synthesizing new beliefs (Wikipedia On-Line).

One current initiative involves the United States Institute of Peace which became a reality after President Ronald Reagan signed the United States Institute of Peace Act in 1984. The institute was created by Congress as a non-partisan, federal institution that would work to prevent or end world-wide conflict. USIP works in more than 30 countries, and publishes works on interfaith dialogue, recognizing that many worldwide conflicts have religious underpinnings or overtones (Ibid.).

Campus-Joy – 8:17 pm: It is often said that negative actions are not the point of treatment, but rather, the focus of intervention should be in the mindset of the individual. I can certainly see the global advantage of world religions being at peace with one another, but what is the "cost" of such an accomplishment? By cost I mean, "Who will give? Who will take? How much? What limits will each world religion place on the compromises it will accept?"

Square-Away – 8:21 pm: Well, I can clearly see how a paradigm shift of the New Spirituality would give impetus to these global goals. Who would have thought our little blogging sessions could pull aside the masks and allow us to see such deceptive single focus? If my trust in the Lord were not so galvanized, I'd feel like a beached sailor right now!

Laurie – 8:23 pm: I'll add a few more initiatives that are on the global table:

Dr. Hans Kung, a Professor of Ecumenical Theology and President of the Foundation for a Global Ethic has formulated an often-noted quotation: "There will be no peace among the nations without peace among the religions. There will be no peace among the religions without dialogue among the religions" (Ibid.).

Tony Blair's 2010 initiative to focus on North America as the first target of his faith-based operations has gone very well, after developing relationships with a network of influential faith leaders and organizations. Blair's advisory council of faith leaders included Rick Warren, Pastor of Saddleback Church and David Coffey, president of the Baptist World Alliance (The Guardian On-Line).

There is concern on both sides of the conservative/liberal fence regarding interfaith progress toward a global religion. This, of course, would depend on the willingness of worldwide religions to meet together on shared values and beliefs, while placing their individual beliefs "on the shelf" for now.

For me, the jargon used in Tony Blair's initiative strikes home. I'm a retired teacher who well remembers the early 1990's, when teachers were advised to place their individual beliefs regarding education "on the shelf" for now. We were supposed to be flattered that we were called upon to be "change agents" in our classrooms. Actually, we were thrust into a game of "dumbing down" the students, only to prepare the way for more government intervention to "fix our country's crisis in education." This saga has plowed on now for two decades, spending countless millions of dollars, and "testing children" right out of a love for learning, only to reach the final declaration that we must "nationalize" education in the United States. Of course, we all know that "nationalizing" is really a short-lived predecessor to "globalizing."

<u>Brother Carviss</u> – 8:38 pm: Thank you, Laurie, for sharing something so obviously near to your heart. So many facets of our study have a familiar tone, don't they? Here is another initiative for the Interfaith Movement:

Muslims and Christians together comprise over half of the world's population. It is believed that any future world peace depends on peace between Muslims and Christians. In response to Pope Benedict XVI's Regensburg address of September 13, 2006, Muslims of all denominations and schools of thought joined together to answer the Pope, and indicated two shared values which exists between Muslims and Christians: love of the One God, and love of the neighbor. Muslims then invited Christians to come together with them on the basis of what is common to us, and that which is most essential to the faith and practice of the two religions: The Two Commandments of

Love. This invitation is known as "A Common Word Between Us and You" (A Common Word On-Line).

Does anyone hear an echo of "love and oneness?"

Not-So-Fast – 8:44 pm: I actually went to work on joining you all for this topic. Here is a resolution that actually got passed by the U.N. the next month after it was proposed!

In September of 2010, King Abdullah addressed the Plenary Session of the 65th General Assembly of the United Nations in New York City. It was emphasized that a strong, central role for the U.N. was essential to success in "A Common Word Between Us and You." King Abdullah spoke of the importance of resisting forces of division that spread mistrust and misunderstanding. He reminded members of the U.N. that cooperation between Muslims and Christians was essential to world peace, and that shared commandments to love God and neighbor needs support. King Abdullah and his delegation introduced a draft resolution for an annual World Interfaith Harmony Week when the world's people could express teachings of their own faith about tolerance and world peace (Ibid.).

The resolution for an annual World Interfaith Harmony Week was adopted by the United Nations on October 20, 2010. The first week of February, 2011, was proclaimed the first annual week to celebrate World Interfaith Harmony (United Nations On-Line).

Square-Away – 8:54 pm: Hector did you have to go to Davy Jones' Locker to get that juicy bit of info? Most would say that a resolution could never pass and be placed into action so quickly. I think we may see a lot of government proposals and secret deals begin to move at breakneck speed. Just sayin', that's all!

Brother Carviss – 8:57 pm: On another note, and a highly important one: In the spring of 2011, the White House launched a new program called "The President's Interfaith and Community Service Campus Challenge." The goal was to advance interfaith cooperation and community service in higher education. The focus was to accomplish a familiar aspiration: coming together as a united world interfaith system in order to meet the needs of society. In 2012, URI will host 534 Cooperation Circles in 79 countries. URI's Global Youth Network has more than 500 youth groups and organizations committed to interreligious peace (United Religions Initiative On-Line).

Under the canopy of the "United Religions Initiative," (founded in 2000), the URI Young Leaders Program offers quality trainings to youth all over the world. One example of a training in October, 2010:

Europe Region: Youth leaders, serving students from high school through college, from Europe, North America and the Middle East met in Istanbul, Turkey to discuss some significant challenges they were collectively facing in their own regions. One huge threat was the possibility of religious extremism and the rise of Islamophobia. These high school and college students learned skills which helped those from the Middle East to participate effectively in the region's uprisings just a few months later (Ibid.).

Campus-Joy – 9:05 pm: Wow! This is coming home! A couple of years ago, one of my classmates in "World Religions" was invited to participate in the URI Young Leaders Program – Europe Region. He returned to school, noticeably quiet and pensive. He shared from his experience, but each time I sensed a strange detachment between him and us in the class. I'm hoping one day he can share his heart without restraint.

Laurie – 9:09 pm: Knowing that I'm a retired teacher, you'll understand why I'm bringing the next initiative. As this massive global paradigm shift rushes to become reality, we need to think clearly. While there is effort to bring all social strata and age groups to the table, targeted focus must be on the youth. The young mind is an open page, waiting to be imprinted and colored with a particular mindset. As students move into higher education, the game compellingly turns to discrediting all former values with disdain, then offering a wholesale alternative – postmodern values. Evidence of this strategy is found within the following URI elementary and middle school activities, complete with lesson plans. God, help us, and forgive us for our lethargic ways!

Following are a number of lesson titles from the United Religions Initiative for kids. Some will also include the classroom objective for that lesson:

- The Preamble, Purpose and Principles of the URI

    "We, people of diverse religions, spiritual expressions and indigenous traditions throughout the world, hereby establish the United Religions Initiative to promote enduring, daily interfaith cooperation, to end religiously motivated violence and to create cultures of peace, justice and healing for the Earth and all living beings. ... "

- Creating a Multicultural Shrine

    Objective: For students to connect spirituality to themselves. To share with others what is important to them. To create a sacred space within the classroom.

- Meditation Practice

    Objective: To give students a couple of quiet minutes out of their hectic day. To allow for some brief quiet reflection. To teach students the basics of meditation or silent prayer. To increase student's comfort with being quiet and not always being distracted. Students may be asked to write in their Learning Logs during or after meditation. (Meditation time can

- Vocabulary Word Games (Some words used: deity, nirvana, meditation, Brahman, Koran, Atman, mosque, idol, atonement, Jihad, Diaspora, Guru, polytheism, Monotheism, Messiah)
- Wicca
- New Age
- Judaism: Background, Basic Beliefs and Sacred Texts
- Islam: Basic Beliefs
- Hinduism: Background, Basic Beliefs and Sacred Texts
- Buddhism: Basic Beliefs
- Visual Voyages: Seeing Sacred Spaces
- World Religions

    Students join to discuss topics such as:

    - "What is religion?"
    - "What is a spiritual tradition?"
    - "A way of explaining the mysteries of life, i.e. why there is life and death, and what happens when people die;"
    - "A way of describing a dimension beyond the physical world – the spiritual world;"
    - "A way of explaining how to lead a good life on Earth and in an afterlife."

    (United Religions Initiative On-Line)

So, we can easily see that United Religions Initiative has it all sewed up: our kids, from elementary through college, have extensive opportunities to study many religions and learn a type of cultural relativity (any person's religious beliefs are right for them in their own cultures since all paths lead to God). Notice that these are activities planned for school classrooms!

Brother Carviss – 9:15 pm: Is there any question as to how late on the prophetic clock we're moving? Does anyone notice the speed with which so many areas are coming into fruition? Let's not be among the "Hezekiahs" who are only concerned about the peace and truth of their own generation, being apathetic to even their own children's plight (Isaiah 39:6-8)! Our Lord Jesus Christ encouraged his disciples, "Now when these things begin to happen, look up and lift up your heads, because your redemption draws near" (Luke 21:28).

Laurie, please begin with the "Sleight-Of-Hand" vocabulary terms for this session.

Laurie – 9:18 pm: "New Jerusalem"

From Hubbard's "Christ" in *The Revelation*:

"It is the human community as a collectivity of natural Christs" (Hubbard, op. cit. 258).

"In the new Jerusalem, humanity and God are one" (Ibid. 286).

"Remember, Satan is either consumed by fire or by love. In the New Jerusalem, there is no illusion of separation" (Ibid. 297).

Campus-Joy – 9:23 pm: "New Jerusalem"

"And I saw a new heaven and a new earth, for the first heaven and the first earth had passed away. Also there was no more sea. Then I, John, saw the holy city, New Jerusalem, coming down out of heaven from

God, prepared as a bride adorned for her husband" (Revelation 21:1-2).

<u>Laurie</u> – 9:28 pm: "Overcomers"

" 'Love' and 'peace' will prevail when 'fear' and 'separation' are overcome. 'Overcomers,' according to the New Age/New Gospel, are those who have overcome 'fear' and 'separation' by recognizing they are part of God and 'at-one' with all creation" (Smith, False, op. cit. 96).

"It is essential at the moment of infusion of empathy that you overcome all fear of separation from God. This overcoming of fear in a whole planetary experience is an irresistible force. No being can resist it" (Hubbard, op. cit. 244-245).

<u>Campus-Joy</u> – 9:33 pm: "Overcomers"

"Do not be overcome by evil, but overcome evil with good" (Romans 12:21).

"He who overcomes shall inherit all things, and I will be his God and he shall be My son" (Revelation 21:7).

> Then I heard a loud voice saying in heaven, "Now salvation, and strength, and the kingdom of our God, and the power of His Christ have come, for the accuser of our brethren who accused them before our God day and night, has been cast down. And they overcame him by the blood of the Lamb and by the word of their testimony, and they did not love their lives to the death" (Revelation 12:10-11).

<u>Laurie</u> – 9:40 pm: "Co-creative"

From Hubbard's "Christ" in *The Revelation*:

> Here we are, now poised either on the brink of destruction greater than the world has ever seen – a destruction which will cripple planet Earth forever and release only the few to go on – or on the threshold of global co-creation wherein each person on Earth will be attracted to participate in his or her own evolution to godliness (Hubbard, op. cit. 174).

<u>Campus-Joy</u> – 9:44 pm: "Co-creative"

> In the beginning was the Word, and the Word was with God, and the Word was God. He was in the beginning with God. All things were made through Him, and without Him nothing was made. In Him was life, and the life was the light of men. And the light shines in the darkness, and the darkness did not comprehend it (John 1:1-5).

<u>Laurie</u> – 950 pm: "Empathy"

From Hubbard's "Christ" in *The Revelation*:

"As the Planetary Smile ripples through the nervous systems of earth and the Instant of Co-operation begins, empathy floods the feelings of the whole body of Earth, separateness is over, and I appear to all of you at once" (Hubbard, op. cit. 245).

> As this joy flashes through the nervous systems of the most sensitive people on Earth, it will create a psycho-magnetic field of empathy, which will align the next wave of people in synchrony, everywhere on Earth. This massive, sudden empathic alignment will cause a shift in the consciousness of Earth (Ibid. 243).

<u>Campus-Joy</u> – 9:58 pm: "Empathy"

"Rejoice with those who rejoice, and weep with those who weep. Be of the same mind toward one another. Do not set your mind on high things, but associate with the humble. Do not be wise in your own opinion" (Romans 12:15-16).

<u>Laurie</u> – 10:02 pm: "Pentecost"

"You are to prepare the way for the alternative to Armageddon, which is the Planetary Pentecost, the great Instant of Co-operation which can transform enough, en masse, to avoid the necessity of the seventh seal being broken" (Hubbard, op. cit. 172-173).

<u>Campus-Joy</u> – 10:06 pm: "Pentecost"

> Now when the Day of Pentecost had fully come, they were all with one accord in one place. And suddenly there came a sound from heaven, as of a rushing mighty wind, and it filled the whole house where they were sitting. Then there appeared to them divided tongues, as of fire, and one sat upon each of them. And they were all filled with the Holy Spirit and began to speak with other tongues, as the Spirit gave them utterance (Acts 2:1-4).

> When He opened the seventh seal, there was silence in heaven for about half an hour. And I saw the seven angels who stand before God, and to them were given seven trumpets. Then another angel, having a golden censer, came and stood at the altar. And he was given much incense, that he should offer it with the prayers of all the saints upon the golden altar which was before the throne. And the smoke of the incense, with the prayers of the saints, ascended before God from the angel's hand. Then the angel took the censer, filled it with fire from the altar, and threw it to the earth. And

there were noises, thunderings, lightnings, and an earthquake (Revelation 8:1-5).

Brother Carviss — 10:12 pm: What a sobering passage on which to end this session. We're learning and walking through the crucible of this age.

Each individual will stand on one side: the question is "on which side?" There is no middle ground!

Next week, our topic will be, "Where Is This Going? Will The Real Church Please Stand Up?" "Sleight-Of-Hand" vocabulary terms for next week are: "Christ: appearing to the whole earth at one time," "Marked with the seal of the living God," "Triumph over Satan," "Self-centeredness," "Only one God," "Word of God made Flesh," and "Your eyes will be opened."

Sources to help prepare for next session are Smith's *False Christ Coming. Does Anybody Care?*, Hubbard's *Revelation*, Walsch's *Friendship With God*, and *Conversations With God*, Books 1, 3.

Until next week, October 4th at 8:00 p.m.

Meryl Carviss (blog host)

@chapter_ten

WHERE IS THIS GOING? WILL THE REAL CHURCH PLEASE STAND UP?

> "And the Lord God of their fathers sent warnings to them by His messengers, rising up early and sending them, because He had compassion on His people and on His dwelling place." (2 Chronicles 36:15)

October 4, 2011 – STUDY FORUM BLOGGERS CHECKED IN:

>Brother Carviss >Laurie >Hannah "Campus-Joy" >Hector "Not-so-Fast" >Will "Square-Away"

Brother Carviss – 8:00 pm: We're coming near the end of this study, my dear bloggers. Our last session will be next week. Let's begin with our "Sleight-Of-Hand" vocabulary for this session, looking at the phrase, "Christ Appearing to the Whole Earth at One Time."

Laurie – 8:03 pm: "Christ Appearing to the Whole Earth at One Time"

From Hubbard's "Christ" in *The Revelation*:

> At the moment of cosmic contact, I will appear to you both through inner experience and through external communication in your mass media – the nervous system of the world. You will all feel, hear, and see my presence at one instant in time, each in your own way (Hubbard, op. cit. 245).

Campus-Joy – 8:07 pm: "Christ Appearing to the Whole Earth at One Time"

The words of Jesus Christ:

> Then the sign of the Son of Man will appear in heaven, and then all the tribes of the earth will mourn, and they will see the Son of Man coming on the clouds of heaven with power and great glory. And He will send His angels with a great sound of a trumpet, and they will gather together His elect from the four winds, from one end of heaven to the other (Matthew 24:30-31).

<u>Laurie</u> – 8:11 pm: "Marked with the Seal"

From Hubbard's "Christ" in *The Revelation*: "Those with the seal of the living God on their foreheads will be with Christ at the time of the Transformation" (Hubbard, op. cit. 190).

<u>Campus-Joy</u> – 8:14 pm: "Marked with the Seal"

> And he causes all, both small and great, rich and poor, free and slave, to receive a mark on their right hand or on their foreheads, and that no one may buy or sell except one who has the mark or the name of the beast, or the number of his name. Here is wisdom. Let him who has understanding calculate the number of the beast, for it is the number of a man: His number is 666 (Revelation 13:16-18).

<u>Laurie</u> – 8:18 pm: "Triumph over Satan"

From Hubbard's "Christ" in *The Revelation*: "Your triumph over Satan, that is, over the illusion of separation, will be a victory for the universal community" (Hubbard, op. cit. 193).

<u>Campus-Joy</u> – 8:22 pm: "Triumph over Satan"

"O Death, where is your sting: O Hades, where is your victory? The sting of death is sin, and the strength of sin is the law. But thanks be to God, who gives us the victory through our Lord Jesus Christ" (1 Corinthians 15:55-57).

"For whatever is born of God overcomes the world. And this is the victory that has overcome the world – our faith. Who is he who overcomes the world, but he who believes that Jesus is the Son of God" (1 John 5:4-5)?

Laurie – 8:28 pm: "Self-centeredness"

From Hubbard's "Christ" in *The Revelation*:

> The fundamental regression is self-centeredness, or the illusion that you are separate from God. I "make war" on self-centeredness. It shall surely be overcome. The child must become the adult. Human must become Divine. That is the law (Hubbard, op. cit. 233).

"At the co-creative stage of evolution, one self-centered soul is like a lethal cancer cell in a body: deadly to itself and to the whole" (Ibid. 255).

"The selection process will exclude all who are exclusive. The selection process assures that only the loving will evolve to the stage of co-creator" (Ibid. 303).

Campus-Joy – 8:39 pm: "Self-centeredness"

"For I say, through the grace given to me, to everyone who is among you, not to think of himself more highly than he ought to think, but to think soberly, as God has dealt to each one a measure of faith" (Romans 12:3).

"And let us consider one another in order to stir up love and good works" (Hebrews 10:24).

Laurie – 8:43 pm: "Only One God"

Direct quotes from Walsch's "God" in *Friendship with God*:

"There is only one message that can change the course of human history forever, end the torture, and bring you back to God. That message is The New Gospel: WE ARE ALL ONE" (Walsch 373).

"There is only One of Us. You and I are One" (Ibid. 23).

"There are a thousand paths to God, and every one gets you there" (Ibid. 357).

Campus-Joy – 8:50 pm: "Only One God"

"There is one body and one Spirit, just as you were called in one hope of your calling; one Lord, one faith, one baptism; one God and Father of all ... " (Ephesians 4:4-6).

"Thomas said to Him, 'Lord, we do not know where you are going, and how can we know the way?'"
"Jesus said to him, 'I am the way, the truth, and the life. No one comes to the Father except through Me' " (John 14:5-6).

Laurie – 8:55 pm: "Word of God made Flesh"

From Walsch's "God:" "You are *already* a God. *You simply do not know it*" (CWG Book1, 202).

"You are the Creator and the Created" (CWG Book 3, 350).

"You are quite literally, the Word of God, made flesh" (FWG 395).

<u>Campus-Joy</u> – 9:00 pm: "Word of God made Flesh"

> And the Word became flesh and dwelt among us, and we beheld His glory, the glory as of the only begotten of the Father, full of grace and truth. John bore witness of Him and cried out, saying, "This was He of whom I said, 'He who comes after me is preferred before me, for He was before me.' And of His fullness we have all received, and grace for grace" (John 1:14-16).

<u>Laurie</u> – 9:04 pm: "Your Eyes will be Opened"

Quotes from Hubbard's "Christ" in *The Revelation*:

> You are to provide the opportunity for a planetary signal wherein each person who chooses life over death can register that decision visibly - a coming to witness before the world (Hubbard, op. cit. 302).

> Each shall be 'sealed' with the seal of the living God. This means that they shall be marked, visibly identified, first to themselves, then to others. This means that their inner eye in the forehead will be fully opened by this touch, henceforth awakening them from the womb of self-centeredness (Ibid. 149).

<u>Campus-Joy</u> – 9:10 pm: "Your Eyes will be Opened"

> Now the serpent was more cunning than any beast of the field which the Lord God had made. And he said to the woman, "Has God indeed said, 'You shall not eat of every

tree of the garden?"' And the woman said to the serpent, "We may eat the fruit of the trees of the garden; but of the fruit of the tree which is in the midst of the garden, God has said, 'You shall not eat it, nor shall you touch it, lest you die.'" And the serpent said to the woman, "You will not surely die. For God knows that in the day you eat of it your eyes will be opened, and you will be like God, knowing good and evil" (Genesis 3:1-5).

<u>Brother Carviss</u> – 9:14 pm: Many thanks to Laurie and Hannah, who have diligently prepared and led our sections on "Sleight-Of-Hand" vocabulary. It's really uncanny to witness the shared vocabulary with such opposing descriptions and references.

<u>Not-So-Fast</u> – 9:16 pm: I think it was the "Sleight-Of-Hand" vocabulary that mostly got my attention and made me think. Now, I see things from a much different perspective than before I accepted the Lord. I have such a freedom to really consider God's Word, and an understanding of it that I could never have expected.

<u>Square-Away</u> – 9:20 pm: Paul encourages the young Timothy, as I do you, Hector: "Be diligent to present yourself approved to God, a worker who does not need to be ashamed, rightly dividing the word of truth" (2 Timothy 2:15).

Paul was talking about being faithful to study God's Word, and to rightly divide it (meaning to correctly understand and teach it). Stay close to God's Word, Hector, and you'll be amazed at how God will use you to draw others to Him.

<u>Brother Carviss</u> – 9:25 pm: This evening, I'd like to have some informal conversation as we review and also look ahead to where all this is going. I'll generally lead in discussion, and please be free to join in with questions or comments.

A question I'd like us to consider: Who are we modeling? If our Father had wanted us to know how to get closer to Him, how to hear him better, how to enjoy the ultra elation of His presence through meditation and contemplative prayer, would he not have told us about it in His Word? Wouldn't He have modeled that behavior with directions about how to enter this most important level of consciousness?

Laurie – 9:29 pm: What strikes me here is that, as we meditate and seek the one word or phrase to use in entering that inner silence, whose modeling are we imitating: Jesus Christ of Nazareth or the New Age Spirituality? Even though the experience of contemplative prayer sometimes leads one to a feeling of joy, peace, and security, we must consider that Satan, himself, often appears as an Angel of Light. He knows scripture, and can quote it to deliver a "tailor made" word of encouragement, direction, and a euphoric sense of having spent time with the one, true living God. Let's keep in mind that the overwhelming description of Satan's activity is "deception."

Campus-Joy – 9:34 pm: At the halting of construction at the tower of Babel, I've often wondered why the unified language was confused, and made into various languages by the Lord?

Brother Carviss – 9:36 pm: Hannah, I think it had to do with halting the people's pride regarding what great things they could accomplish, without God's counsel. I also think that Satan knew if He could ever get all the inhabitants of earth to agree together (global spiritual unity), that they would give allegiance to Satan, the one who often guided their meditation. If Satan is ever able to get all humanity to agree in worship of him, through meditation, then He will be like a god (with his throne on the earth among all of "god's people.") Father God smashed that demonic plan in Babel, and His Word says He will smash that plan in the "end time." "And the devil, who deceived them, was cast into the lake of fire and brimstone where the beast and the false prophet are. And they will be tormented day and night forever and ever"

(Revelation 20:10). Just as in Noah's ark, in Joseph's Egypt, in Daniel's lions' den, in Job's loss, in Paul's imprisonment …. God will take His own out of the diabolical plan of Satan for this earth, and the times of Satan will find their end.

Square-Away – 9:40 pm: How will Satan and all of humanity be one, with all worship going to him?

Brother Carviss – 9:42 pm: In the spirit world, the Holy Spirit is not sharing meditation "tabernacles" with the demonic realm. Therefore, if all meditation goes on in the spiritual domain, could it not be that Satan is donning his "angel-of-light-get-up" to deceive Christians into believing they are communicating with the true God? The real test will come at "selection time."

Laurie – 9:45 pm: Just to get a little quantum physics in here, do you all remember that quantum particles and the behavior of such, are only seen when visualized by an observer? In the quantum world, observers always have an influence on the "observed." Now, try this theory on for size: when entering the spirit world via meditation and contemplative prayer, it is by the observer's desire to "see" or "visualize" into the spirit world that entities in that realm are actualized for interaction. The spirit world cannot initiate the first contact. Spirits in that realm can only interact with a willing observer. This theory, however, does not apply to the Holy Spirit – who is the personal gift given to all those who believe and accept Jesus Christ as their personal Savior (Acts 2:38).

Brother Carviss – 9:49 pm: Well, Laurie, that's really putting quantum physics to the test, isn't it? We'll get to ask Jesus about that theory one day. Let's think now about the time in history in which we live, and what we can see as the future unfolds.

We understand that it is not for us to know the date or the hour when Jesus Christ will return for His own, but we can prepare as we observe many prophesied events coming together. "But of that day and hour no one knows, no, not even the angels of heaven, but My Father only .... Therefore you also be ready, for the Son of Man is coming at an hour when you do not expect Him" (Matthew 24:36, 44).

Further, Jesus taught an object lesson through a tree: "...Look at the fig tree, and all the trees. When they are already budding, you see and know for yourselves that summer is now near. So you, likewise, when you see these things happening, know that the kingdom of God is near" (Luke 21:29-31).

We also know that perilous times will come when the Church of Jesus Christ, world-wide, will suffer persecution and many will be martyred. "But know this, that in the last days perilous times will come" (2 Timothy 3:1). And, "Yes, and all who desire to live godly in Christ Jesus will suffer persecution" (2 Timothy 3:12).

Furthermore, we can look all around to observe a great "falling away" as countless churches grow tepid and even intolerant to the commands of Holy Scripture. "Another gospel" is not just easing in on the horizon, but rather is invading with the force and intent of a tsunami. As one questions the changes in basic beliefs of the emerging church, it soon becomes evident that a New Spirituality is taking shape. This spirituality often denies sin, the presence of hell, and the need for individuals to come to Jesus Christ with a repentant heart in order to receive forgiveness, salvation, and sanctification. There are multiple theologies, doctrines, and practices among the wide span of emergent communities. Some make a difference in the terms "emergent" and "emerging," but the general propositions and praxes inevitably find the same root.

As one explores further, he is aware that there is a deep and profound base for this new, emerging movement. There is a new spirituality which paints a vivid picture of current life on this earth with no sin, no hell, no heaven (except for humans bringing hell and heaven to this earth now). There is no need of salvation, for all belong to the body of Christ now. Looking further into these strange "Christian" teachings, one will find that the authentic root is deeply imbedded in New Age Spirituality.

Square-Away – 9:58 pm: Now, where is this headed? It seems we are hastily moving on the path toward the New Age One World Plan. This plan will eventually "select" those who will proceed into the place of co-creators, and it will reject those who are holding up New Age progress by standing firmly on the biblical truth of salvation by grace, through faith in Jesus Christ alone. The intention is to re-educate or eliminate the people who are holding up the ancient/future plan of the Ruler of Darkness.

While many thought the New Age movement was quieted down nearly to silence, events of the past decade have ushered an opportunity for the plans of darkness to rush in, almost unnoticed in the global chase for peace at almost any cost.

Have we been left here without any foreknowledge of what is happening? Absolutely not! The Word of God explicitly warns us of the "falling away" of the church as the time for Christ's return approaches.

Laurie – 10:08 pm: Then, why do we see such a "silent church?" As we borrow these questions from Warren Smith, we're in a dire situation to attempt answering these indictments.

- Why is there almost no call for spiritual discernment within the church (except to warn believers not to be deceived into doubting their appointed Christian leaders)?
- Why is spiritual experience taking precedence over spiritual discernment?
- Why are there so few warnings about a counterfeit New Age/New Spirituality movement that maligns the person of Jesus Christ and threaten the lives of His followers?
- Why is "new revelation" in many ministries starting to supersede God's written Word?

- Why are Christians only being prepared for blessings and not for persecution?
- Is the "God of forces" in the process of preparing a deceived church for the "Planetary Pentecost?"
- Has anyone wondered whether this same "Force" may be counterfeiting the Holy Spirit in churches and may be producing revivals and moves of God that are not really revivals or moves of God at all?
- Have we put our faith and trust in Christian "leaders" rather than in God?
- Have we prayed to God that we would not be deluded or deceived? (Smith, False, op. cit. 119-120).

All these questions bring up a controversial, yet valid, point. If the church is only prepared for blessing, revival, and a Rapture taking place before any global persecution begins, then will the church be ready, if called upon, to take a stand during the early times of world wide selection, re-education, and persecution? If, on the other hand, we are ready for persecution, then we will surely be ready to be taken up to meet our Lord in the air and to ever be with our Lord.

> For the Lord himself will descend from heaven with a shout, with the voice of an archangel, and with the trumpet of God. And the dead in Christ will rise first. Then we who are alive and remain shall be caught up together with them in the clouds to meet the Lord in the air. And thus we shall always be with the Lord (1 Thessalonians 4:16-17).

A diluted gospel will lead to global ecumenical unity – the only ones not fitting in are those refusing to drop the exclusiveness of Jesus Christ, the one and only begotten of God, who has paid the debt for our sin. As we confess our sinful natures to Him and surrender to His will, we will receive salvation and righteousness in our lives. It seems to me that it is time for the Western church to get prepared to stand in the face of persecution, and to ask some soul-searching questions.

Brother Carviss – 10: 15 pm: With those humbling questions, we'll say good-night. Next session, I'd like to ask each of you to share something you've read or viewed that applies to the topic: "Where Do We Go From Here?"

Until next week, October 11th at 8:00 p.m.

Meryl Carviss (blog host)

@chapter_eleven

WHERE DO WE GO FROM HERE?

"The single step of a courageous individual is not to take part in the lie. One word of truth out-weighs the world." (Alexander Solzhenitsyn)

October 11, 2011 – STUDY FORUM BLOGGERS CHECKED IN:

>Brother Carviss >Laurie >Hannah "Campus-Joy" >Hector "Not-so-Fast" >Will "Square-Away"

Brother Carviss – 8:00 pm: Heaven is so worth waiting for!

A city described as:

- Measuring 1377 miles long, wide, and high;
- Illuminated by the glory of God, and Jesus is its light;
- Walls of jasper, clear as crystal;
- Streets of pure gold, like transparent glass;
- Twelve gates, each made of a single pearl;
- Perfect healing with the tree of life in its midst;
- God wipes away every tear: no more death, nor sorrow, nor crying, nor pain;
- No evil present.

In addition to all the wonders above, the purest treasure is seeing our Lord face to face, knowing His Name is on our foreheads, that we're truly home, and we will reign with our King Jesus forever and ever (Revelation 21-22).

Having Jesus' Name eternally on our foreheads is a sharp contrast to the atrocity of bearing the mark of the beast, the antichrist, the father of lies on our foreheads eternally! How blessed we are to know the Truth, the Truth which sets us free (John 8:32). We know the Truth because Jesus, The Word of God, gave us forewarning of what shall take place so that we could be ready to walk through that time in confidence and trust in Him. There will come that day when all the mystery will be revealed, and the eternal Truth of who is the King of Kings and Lord of Lords will be proclaimed forever – yes, in heaven (Revelation 19:16)! As Moses, we can then say that we chose rather to suffer affliction with the people of God than to enjoy the passing pleasures of sin. We esteemed our reviling, because of Jesus, to be greater riches than the treasures in Egypt (or America) for we were looking to the reward. By faith we, like Moses, forsook the present security, not even fearing the wrath of the system; for then we endured as seeing Jesus Christ, who is invisible (Hebrews 11:25-27).

Square-Away – 8:10 pm: Well, Brother Carviss, that "intro to the conclusion" has put fire in my bones already! My old seafarer's heart is burdened with the probability that some dear mates following our blog may still be waiting to take the step of faith that our Hector took a few weeks ago. Right now, this old Bluejacket would like to "square away" the path to accepting the Lord's free gift of salvation to any who are ready:

If you are not a follower of the Lord Jesus Christ, of the Bible, this would be a perfect time for you to look into the Bible, God's Holy Word, and find the truth of life eternal. Because of man's sin (beginning in the garden of Eden), he created an impassable gulf between us and Father God. However God, in His wisdom, pure love, and mercy provided a bridge for that gulf. His name is Jesus Christ, the only begotten Son of God the Father. Born of a virgin, Jesus lived a perfect life on this earth, spent three years in concentrated ministry with his disciples, then lay down His life to pay the debt we could never pay. In doing this, Jesus secured the passage across that bridged gulf. Our part is simply to believe that Jesus Christ is truly the Son of God, to be willing to repent of a sinful life of unbelief, thus allowing an "about face" in our mind, heart, and actions. Then confess you believe that Jesus Christ came in the flesh, and dwelt among us humans, enduring the cross and rose again, to secure heaven for us. Next, invite Jesus to be your Savior and Lord, and to take His rightful place in your heart. Jesus called this the "born again" experience. Jesus also modeled baptism to fulfill all righteousness. These scriptures will guide you in this experience: Romans 3:23, Romans 3:10, Romans 6:23, Romans 5:8, Romans 10:9-10, Romans 10: 13, I John 5:12-13, and Acts 2:41.

Brother Carviss – 8:18 pm: Thank you, Will. You were right on with your invitation to accept Christ as Savior and Lord. I'd encourage any who made that decision and commitment to begin reading and studying the Bible. The Gospel of John in the New Testament is an ideal place to begin reading.

Campus–Joy – 8:22 pm: I have been thinking about this verse, "Yes, and all who desire to live godly in Christ Jesus will suffer persecution (2 Timothy 3:12). So I'd like to share an anonymous writing that has deeply touched my heart:

AM I A PART OF THE DEAD LIVING OR THE LIVING DEAD?

As I enjoy each day in the "land of the free and the home of the brave," I must ask myself: "Do I really live in the land of the bound and the home of the coward?"

QUESTION: Am I part of the "dead living" or the "living dead?"

If my security in this country were suddenly and terminally interrupted, would I remain a "closet Christian" – not denying the Lord in my heart – but quietly going along with the political and cultural changes in order to spare my family, myself, my portfolio from being a target of disclosure?

QUESTION: Am I part of the "dead living" or the "living dead?"

If it were against the law to meet with fellow Christians and punishable by loss of job, imprisonment, or even death – would I secretly meet with brothers and sisters in Christ to worship, encourage, and evangelize – or would I secretly "hold up" with my family in our own home and let no one suspect I was a Christian?

QUESTION: Am I part of the "dead living" or the "living dead?"

If I could be hauled off to a forced labor camp of intensely degrading and threatening conditions for sharing Christ with any person in my community, would I risk losing all just to tell one person about my Lord?

QUESTION: Am I part of the "dead living" or the "living dead?"

If, given the choice of witnessing the torture and murder of a close family member – or of denying Christ (while still secretly believing in Him in my heart) – which would I choose?

QUESTION: Am I part of the "dead living" or the "living dead?"

After witnessing the torturous murder of my spouse and children, would I allow Father God to move in my heart in a forgiveness which would compel me to share the truth of the Gospel with those who have taken my loved ones?

QUESTION: Am I part of the "dead living" or the "living dead?"

Facing none of the previous scenarios at this time, can I come above my selfish pride and fear to prayerfully watch for open doors, then boldly walk through those doors to share Christ with a neighbor, a relative, a co-worker, an enemy?

QUESTION: Am I part of the "dead living" or the "living dead?

<u>Laurie</u> – 8:40 pm: Thanks, Hannah! This is a sobering chain of questions for the people of God. As you shared from 2 Timothy 3:12, we will be persecuted if we are bold enough to really live godly lives. I heard a missionary once say that if we are not enduring any persecution, we might need to look at the quality of our lives. So it seems to me that we should expect to receive persecution, as Jesus Himself told us that if He was persecuted, we should know that we will also walk that trail (John 15:20).

We can also know that we are not isolated in persecution, but that we are joined by godly people through the ages who chose to follow Jehovah God.

> Beloved, do not think it strange concerning the fiery trial which is to try you, as though some strange thing happened to you; but rejoice to the extent that you partake of Christ's sufferings, that when His glory is revealed, you may also be glad with exceeding joy. If you are reproached for the name of Christ, blessed are you for the Spirit of glory and of God rests upon you. On their part He is blasphemed, but on your part He is glorified (1 Peter 4:12-14).

Hebrews 11 is a power packed chapter on faith, particularly giving the history of many authentic men and women of God who stood firm in the trials they faced. I love how Hebrews 12 begins:

> Therefore we also, since we are surrounded by so great a cloud of witnesses, let us lay aside every weight, and the sin which so easily ensnares us and let us run with endurance the

race that is set before us, looking unto Jesus, the author and finisher of our faith who for the joy that was set before Him endured the cross, despising the shame, and has sat down at the right hand of the throne of God (Hebrews 12:1-2).

Not-So-Fast – 8:50 pm: I'm not sharing much this evening. I hope you all don't mind, but I'm just soaking in all this weighty stuff that is so new to me. It is heavy to take in, but I remember the words of Jesus which someone gave me, "Take My yoke upon you and learn from Me, for I am gentle and lowly in heart, and you will find rest for your souls. For My yoke is easy and My burden is light" (Matthew 11: 29-30).

I take that to mean that we may walk a steep, rocky cliff, but Jesus takes the hard part and leaves us with what we can handle, in Him. Mostly, I like the reality of having rest for my soul!

Square-Away – 8:54 pm: Now here's a passage that makes me want to weigh anchor and start sailing, " .... that I may know Him and the power of His resurrection, and the fellowship of His sufferings, being conformed to His death, if by any means, I may attain to the resurrection from the dead" (Philippians 3:10-11).

In my words, if I want to know the power of Christ's resurrection, then I must also know what it was for Christ to suffer, and I must be willing to tread the same path as He trod.

Brother Carviss – 8:59 pm: One of my most respected brothers in the faith is Richard Wurmbrand, a Romanian pastor who spent fourteen years in Communist prisons. He regularly faced months of solitary confinement, years of periodic physical torture, continually cold and hungry, along with the agony of mental cruelty and brainwashing. Pastor Wurmbrand's crime was his non-budging belief in Jesus Christ and his public witness of his faith. He and thousands of others met "underground" in homes or in the woods, or sometimes preaching on the streets, with a single focus to bring others to Christ, regardless of the consequences. In a *Voice of the Martyrs* publication, *The Triumphant*

Church, Pastor Wurmbrand gives some phenomenal instruction for Christians who will face persecution. His thoughts and admonitions:

- Suffering cannot be avoided in the underground church;
- Preparation for underground work begins by studying "sufferology" and "martyrology." This means not only expecting to suffer for Christ, but know how to do it successfully, without giving in;
- Do not fear prison. Look upon it as just a new assignment given by God;
- The primary reason for torture is to get information regarding others who will then be arrested;
- Whether or not we give in to pressure is determined by the state of our faith: has it remained in the sphere of words, or are we merged with the divine nature of our Lord;
- Knowing it is only the Lord who can strengthen you, if you are truly united with Him, then evil loses its power over you …. It cannot break the Lord Almighty;
- One has to learn to use the things of this world without allowing emotional attachment;
- Learn creative ways to keep your mind active;
- The word "doubt" does not exist for a successful underground worker;
- Quarreling is not permitted in the underground church. Every quarrel brings arrests, beating, torture and perhaps even death;
- Allow torture to strengthen and harden your resolve to be true to God and His people;
- Know that there is a "moment of crisis" during which believers may be very close to giving in to their captors. Once a person successfully passes this "moment of crisis," torture will no longer hold its terror;
- Learn to be silent. Really listen to the burdens of those without Christ that you may win them by your love;

- Memorize as much scripture as possible. This will become the Bible you will read when the written Word of God is no longer available to you (Wurmbrand 5-38).

I love the Bible's prescription for a "gentle servant:"

> And a servant of the Lord must not quarrel but be gentle to all, able to teach, patient, in humility correcting those who are in opposition, if God perhaps will grant them repentance, so that they may know the truth, and that they may come to their senses and escape the snare of the devil, having been taken captive by him to do his will (2 Timothy 2:24-26).

<u>Campus-Joy</u> – 9:20 pm: That passage reminds me of a definition of meekness: "velvet-coated steel." Clearly, those who continue in purity of faith in God Almighty, even when walking into the jaws of persecution, know the gift of meekness!

I'd like to share a few gospel energy bars from John MacArthur:

> So if you are a believer, get into the battle. Fight for the truth. Contend earnestly for the faith. Apostasy is present in the church, and it is probably going to get worse. But we who believe in Jesus Christ have nothing to fear. We are called and loved and kept secure in Him, so we can be supremely confident, even in this era of doubt and uncertainty. Because the One who is truth incarnate---the One whose honor and glory are therefore on the line---is both our Commander and our Protector. And His Word is a formidable weapon (MacArthur, Truth 51).

> So apostasy is a fact of all history, and there is never any kind of armistice in the Truth War. Our generation is certainly no exception to that rule. Some of the greatest threats to truth today come from within the visible church. Apostates are

there in vast abundance---teaching lies, popularizing gross falsehoods, reinventing essential doctrines, and even redefining truth itself. They seem to be everywhere in the evangelical culture today, making merchandise of the gospel (Ibid. 72).

MacArthur also warns that it is folly, as well as disobedience, for today's Christians to throw discernment overboard and, in the name of "love" to unconditionally embrace all who claim to be Christians. John goes further to say that to do that would be to forfeit the entire battle for truth to the enemy (Ibid. 96).

John MacArthur gives us some things to remember:

- Jude urges us to remember what was prophesied (that false teachers would come);
- God is sovereign and has not lost control;
- God is not surprised by apostasy---He prophesied about it;
- Christians, having been warned, should be prepared and vigilant in the Truth War;
- Only willful unbelief can be blamed for the refusal of so many in the church today to heed warnings and be accountable in the Truth War;
- Christians must remain faithful, building themselves up on their most holy faith. This is accomplished by submitting to the spiritual discipline of studying the Word;
- Christians must maintain spiritual stability by "praying in the Holy Spirit;"
- Christians must keep themselves in the love of God by being obedient to the commandments of our Father;
- Keep one's mind on heavenly things, not the things of this world. Jude says to keep "looking for the mercy of our Lord Jesus Christ unto eternal life;"

- Reach out to those who are confused and doubting, those who are convinced and already in the fire, and have mercy on those who are committed to the apostasy in question (Ibid. 175-182).

Brother Carviss – 9:34 pm: As we look back on our ten weeks of blogging on the topic, *Duped! Deception in Graceland*, I can echo the word's from one of our authors, Roger Oakland:

> If I believed for one minute that this movement was just another passing whim or the discontent rumblings that so often accompany young people's search for answers to life, I would never have written this book. And if I did not believe that what we are witnessing with this emerging spirituality lines up with biblical end-time prophecy, you would not be reading these pages. But sad to say, the emerging church is far more than a fleeting fad and more than the complaints of a group of young leaders. It is indeed a "new way of being Christians" and in every conceivable manner, it is striving to bring about a "new reformation." Without a doubt, it will have an "impact on all churches" in the Western world and far beyond. For behind this new kind of church is a well designed strategy and maneuver by the prince of this world, the enemy of our souls, to literally take apart the faith of millions---it will be nothing less than faith undone (Oakland 2).

Laurie – 9:38 pm: Just one final word of encouragement from our Lord Jesus Christ.

Jesus' words, as he gave vital instruction to his disciples:

"These things I have spoken to you, that in Me you may have peace. In the world you will have tribulation; but be of good cheer, I have overcome the world" (John 16:33).

This "overcoming" means that "Jesus has overcome the world's ability" to:

- Define you and your response;
- Move you from the Rock and His power to keep you all the way through this earthly journey and safely across the Jordan one day;
- Deceive you away from God's never failing Light;
- Wear you down and separate you from God's unconditional Love.

May the one true living God bless each one who reads this message!

Brother Carviss, Laurie, Hannah, Hector, and Will

CHAPTER QUESTIONS FOR REFLECTION

@chapter_one

1. Discuss with at least one other person the meaning of this statement:
"We dare not take our Father's forgivenes for granted and treat His ultimate plan of grace as defective."
2. Describe a situation where you would confront apostasy. How would you do that?
3. Roger Oakland said that behind the "New Reformation" is a well designed strategy, maneuvered by the prince of this world, to take apart the faith of millions. Explain what Roger meant by this statement.
4. A few decades ago, it was impossible to imagine what the Bible meant by "false christs" appearing and deceiving many in the last days. Why is the "false christs" terminology much easier to understand today?

@chapter_two

1. Discuss what John MacArthur meant when he spoke of certainty, from a postmodern perspective, as inherently arrogant, intolerant, elitist, oppressive ... and therefore always wrong.
2. What does it mean to be a "co-creator" with God?
3. How does each person on Earth participate in his/her own "evolution to godliness," according to the New Spirituality?

4. What does Rob Bell mean by concluding that the "mystery is actually the truth?"

@chapter_three

1. How has the meaning of mission work changed with the postmodern term, "missiology?"
2. Explain the "convenience" of the postmodern explanation that spiritual explorations can be experienced, but not explained?
3. How is Gnosticism related to the mystery proclaimed today of meditation, contemplative prayer, and the silence?
4. What are some strategies being used in order to permeate today's culture with postmodern thought and agenda?

@chapter_four

1. Journal regarding times you felt the Lord to be "up and out," "down and in," and "in front and behind."
2. Explain why you agree or disagree with Peter Rollins' statement that doubt is a vital part of faith.
3. Elaborate on the apostle Paul's statement, "For the preaching of the cross is to them that perish foolishness; but unto us which are saved it is the power of God."
4. Choose a device of contemplative worship. Then do research and share its origin, as well as historical and current uses of the activity. (Examples: mantra meditation, contemplative prayer, the labyrinth, drumming circle)

@chapter_five

1. Using scripture references, compare and contrast Jesus' dual roles as the Lamb of God and the Lion of Judah.
2. Create a monologue in which you explain to a non-believer how Jesus could become sin for us, and how we can become the righteousness of Christ.

3. Interpret contrasting meanings of the phrase, "being separate," using the New Spirituality connotation and the Holy Bible's implication.
4. How does the New Age concept of "Satan's eternal goal" support the pantheistic claim that "all is one," therefore, each "created being" is god?

@chapter_six

1. What is the significance of "Keep the Promise – 2015?"
2. Create brief entries on Timothy's Notebook to remind him of the significance of each of the apostle Paul's admonitions: "convince," "rebuke," "exhort," "teach."
3. Formulate an infraction list for why Satan was cast out of heaven.
4. Discuss why the New Spirituality refers to "fear," "separation," and "sin" as illusions.

@chapter_seven

1. Develop a sound bite revealing the differences in being "born again," according to both Jesus' explanation and New Spirituality's enlightenment.
2. Defend Square-Away's assessment that Hector enjoys "leaning to the dark side."
3. Share your interpretation of these quotes:

"You were born to be me (the "Christ"]. You were born to be partners with God" (Hubbard, op. cit. 148).

"The church is the body of believers who are conscious of being me [the "Christ"] (Ibid.102).

4. How can the "New Spirituality" be "most ancient?"

@chapter_eight

1. What do you think is behind the caution that new believers should not try contemplative prayer?
2. Find a fellow-believer and do a role play of a conversation between the apostles Peter and James regarding "out of body experiences."
3. Discuss possible outcomes following the "dark night of the soul."
4. How would you advise a new Christian who asks you about New Spirituality's meditation, contemplative prayer, and the silence?

@chapter_nine

1. How would you introduce an Islamic speaker who is about to give a lecture on "A Common Word Between Us and You?"
2. Develop a brochure for parents to highlight, "The President's Interfaith and Community Service Campus Challenge."
3. What is a "change agent" in respect to engineering any paradigm shift? Tell ways you have served as a "change agent."
4. Taking the role of a parent, discuss your beliefs regarding the URI activities being used in your child's classroom.
5. Taking the role of a teacher, discuss your beliefs regarding the URI activities you are required to facilitate in your classroom.

@chapter_ten

Defend or debate the following statements:

1. "There is only One of Us. You and I are One" (Walsch, Friendship, op. cit. 23).
2. "There are a thousand paths to God, and every one gets you there" (Ibid., 357).
3. "You are already a God. You simply do not know it" (Walsch, CWG, Book 1, op. cit. 202).
4. "For whatever is born of God overcomes the world" (1 John 5:4-5).

5. "You are quite literally, the Word of God, made flesh" (Walsch, Friendship, op. cit. 395).

@chapter_eleven

1. Describe the literal heaven, giving at least four characteristics.
2. Are you part of the "dead living" or the "living dead?" Explain.
3. Reveal the meaning of the phrase, " ... we are surrounded by so great a cloud of witnesses ... " (Hebrews 12:1).
4. Model the elements of extreme grace as extracted from Jesus' word of encouragement, "These things I have spoken to you, that in Me you may have peace. In the world you will have tribulation; but be of good cheer, I have overcome the world" (John 16:33).

WORKS CITED

A Course in Miracles: Combined Volume (Glen Ellen, California: Foundation for Inner Peace, 1975, 1992).

*Barbara Marx Hubbard, *The Revelation: A Message of Hope for the New Millennium* (Novato, California: Nataraj Publishing, 1995).

Brian Greene, *Icarus At The Edge Of Time* (New York: Alfred A. Knopf, Publisher, 2008).

Brian Greene, *The Fabric Of The Cosmos* (New York: Random House, Inc., 2004).

Brian D. McLaren, *a Generous Orthodoxy* (Grand Rapids: Zondervan, 2004).

Brian D. McLaren, *A New Kind of Christianity* (New York, New York: HarperOne of Harper-Collins Publishers, 2010).

Brian D. McLaren, *The Church On The Other Side* (Grand Rapids, MI: Zondervan, 2000 edition).

Brian D. McLaren, *The Secret Message of Jesus* (Nashville, Tennessee, W Publishing Group, Thomas Nelson, Inc., 2006).

Carolyn A. Greene, *Castles in the Sand* (Silverton, Oregon: Lighthouse Trails Publishing, 2009).

Dan Kimble, *The Emerging Church* (Grand Rapids: Zondervan 2003).

Donald Miller, *Blue Like Jazz* (Nashville: Zondervan, 2003).

Doug Pagitt, *A Christianity Worth Believing* (Jossey-Bass, A Wiley Imprint, 2008).

Doug Pagitt, *Church Re-Imagined* (Grand Rapids: Zondervan Publishing House, 2005).

Erwin McManus, *The Barbarian Way* (Nashville: Thomas Nelson, 2005).

"Four Stages of Mantra Meditation," *Meditation4Life* website.

John MacArthur, *The MacArthur Study Bible* (Wheaton: Crossway, 2010).

John MacArthur, *The Truth War, Fighting for Certainty in an Age of Deception* (Nashville: Thomas Nelson, 2007).

Kevin DeYoung and Ted Kluck, *Why We're Not Emergent (By Two Guys Who Should Be)* (Chicago: Moody Publishers, 2008).

Leonard Sweet, *Quantum Spirituality: A Postmodern Apologetic* (Dayton: Whaleprints for SpiritVenture Ministries, Inc., 1991, 1994).

Leonard Sweet, *Soul Tsunami* (*Grand Rapids*: Zondervan Publishing House, 2001).

*Marianne Williamson, *Healing the Soul of America: Reclaiming Our Voices as Spiritual Citizens* (NY: Simon & Schuster, 1997, 2000)

Mark Driscoll and Gerry Breshears, *Vintage Jesus: Timeless Answers To Timely Questions* (Wheaton, Illinois: Crossway Books, 2007).

Max Lucado, *In the Eye of the Storm* (Nashville: Thomas Nelson, Inc., 1992).

Milton Martin, John Piper, Richard Wurmbrand, *The Triumphant Church* (Bartlesville: Compiled by The Voice of the Martyrs, 1999).

*Neale Donald Walsch, *Conversations with God: an uncommon dialogue, Book 1* (New York: G.P. Putnam's Sons, Hardcover Edition 1996).

*Neale Donald Walsch, *Conversations with God: an uncommon dialogue*, Book 3 (Charlottesville, Virginia: Hampton Roads, 1998)

*Neale Donald Walsch, *Friendship with God* (New York, NY: G.P. Putnam's Sons, 1999)

Ray Yungen, *A Time of Departing* (Silverton: Lighthouse Trails Publishing, 2nd edition, 2006).

Richard J. Foster, *Celebration of Discipline – The Path to Spiritual Growth* (New York: Harper and Row Publishers, 1978).

Richard J. Foster, *Prayer: Finding The Heart's True Home* (New York: HarperCollins Publishers, 1992).

Richard J. Foster, with Kathryn A. Helmers, *Life With God – Reading the Bible for Spiritual Transformation* (New York: HarperCollins Publishers, 2008).

Rob Bell, *Sex God* (Grand Rapids: Zondervan, 2007).

Rob Bell, *Velvet Elvis* (Grand Rapids: Zondervan, 2005).

Robert Webber, General Editor, *Listening To The Beliefs Of Emerging Churches* (Grand Rapids: Zondervan, 2007).

Roger Oakland, *Faith Undone* (Lighthouse Trails Publishing, 2007).

Warren B. Smith, *A "Wonderful" Deception* (Magalia, CA: Mountain Stream Press, 2009).

Warren B. Smith, False *Christ Coming – Does Anybody Care?* (Magalia, CA: Mountain Stream Press, 2011).

What the Bleep Do We Know!? (Beverly Hills, CA: Twentieth Century Fox Home Entertainment, Inc., 2004).

http://en.wikipedia.org (Wikipedia On-Line)

www.guardian.co.uk (The Guardian On-Line)

http://acommonword.com (A Common Word Between Us and You On-Line)

www.un.org (United Nations On-Line)

www.uri.org/kids (United Religions Initiative On-Line)

www.lighthousetrailsresearch.com/newmissiology.htm (New Missiology On-Line)

www.scriptoriumnovum.com/1/lion.html (Scriptorium Novum On-Line)

*Information and quotations from these works were quoted from Warren B. Smith, *False Christ Coming – Does Anybody Care?* (Magalia, CA: Mountain Stream Press, 2011).

Made in the USA
Charleston, SC
11 February 2012